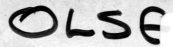

INGE.3.2
Picnic
Inge, William

DATE LOANED	BORROWER'S NAME	DATE RETURNED

PICNIC

A SUMMER ROMANCE

BY WILLIAM INGE

DRAMATISTS PLAY SERVICE INC.

SOUND EFFECT RECORD

Dramatists Play Service can furnish a special sound effect record for use in connection with the production of this play. This record contains the numerous sound effects needed for production, and sells at $4.50, which price includes packing and shipping.

The summer's flower is to the summer sweet . . .

—Shakespeare

Sonnet 94

PICNIC was first produced by The Theatre Guild and Joshua Logan at the Music Box Theatre, New York City on February 19, 1953. It was directed by Joshua Logan, and the scenery and lighting were by Jo Mielziner. The cast was as follows:

HELEN POTTS, *a neighbor* .... Ruth McDevitt
HAL CARTER, *a young vagabond* .... Ralph Meeker
MILLIE OWENS, *a sixteen-year-old girl* .... Kim Stanley
BOMBER, *the paper boy* .... Morris Miller
MADGE OWENS, *a beautiful girl* .... Janice Rule
FLO OWENS, *mother of the girls* .... Peggy Conklin
ROSEMARY SYDNEY, *a school teacher* .... Eileen Heckart
ALAN SEYMOUR, *boy friend of Madge* .... Paul Newman
IRMA KRONKITE, *a school teacher* .... Reta Shaw
CHRISTINE SCHOENWALDER, *a school teacher* .... Elizabeth Wilson
HOWARD BEVANS, *friend of Miss Sydney* .... Arthur O'Connell

SCENE

The action of the play takes place in a small Kansas town in the yard shared by Flo Owens and Helen Potts.

ACT I

Labor Day, early morning.

ACT II

Same day, just before sunset.

ACT III

SCENE 1: Early next morning, before daylight.
SCENE 2: Later the same morning, after sunrise.

4

PICNIC

ACT I

*The action of the play is laid on the porches and in the
yards of two small houses that sit close beside each other
in a small Kansas town. The houses themselves are humble dwellings, built with no other pretension than to pro-
vide shelter for their occupants, but their occupants are
women who have worked hard to keep up an appearance,
so the houses, although they may need a coat of paint, are
kept tidy, and there are colorful slip-covers on the porch
furniture and lush flower-beds at the edge of the porches.
Surrounding the houses are clusters of heavy foliage from
the trees and a stretch of green lawn that levels back, fad-
ing into the horizon. It is a homey scene, marred only by
a sign, hand-painted, tacked to one of the thin little columns on the porch of the house at* R.: *ROOMERS.
The two-story house at* R. *belongs to Mrs. Flo Owens,
a widow lady of about forty, who lives there with her two
young daughters, Madge and Millie. The audience sees
only a section of the house, from the doorstep and front
door extending to the back door, a porch lining all of the
house that we see. There are windows in the house's second story, one of these windows,* U. S., *is the window to
Madge's room. The porch is raised slightly above the
ground, and two long, shallow steps rise from the ground
up to the porch* D. S. R. *Near these steps are matches and
an open pack of cigarettes. Directly beyond the steps a
screen door leads from the porch into the front of the
house—this is the front door. On the porch* R. *of the
steps is a beach chair,* L. *of the steps on the porch is an
armchair, and against the wall of the house, a little* U. S.
on the porch is a bench covered in some bright-flowered

5

material. U. S. on the porch another screen door leads to the kitchen. By the kitchen door a shelf is attached to the wall of the house. Under this shelf is a nail, and on it is Millie's cap. On the porch by the kitchen door is a bottle of milk. In front of the kitchen door the porch juts out a bit, two columns support the roof of the porch here. At C., between the two houses, is a yard with grass. This yard extends D. S. R. in front of Flo's house, at L. it ends where Mrs. Potts' woodshed begins. The yard runs to the back of the stage where, behind the houses, there is a picket fence separating the yard from the alley, which runs along the back of the stage, L. to R. C. in the fence there is a gate leading to the alley. Beyond the yard, the houses and the alley is the panorama of a typical, small Midwestern town, with a church steeple, a grain elevator, a railroad station, a great silo in the center of a cattle ranch, and a few municipal buildings rising out of the level, sloping terrain. C. in the yard, somewhat D. S., is a chair. L. of the chair is an old tree stump. To L. can be seen the back entrance to the house of Mrs. Helen Potts, another but older widow lady, who lives with her aged and invalid mother. A flight of several steps with a railing leads up the side of Mrs. Potts' house and turns into the porch which extends along the U. S. side of the house. Just the beginning of this porch can be seen, the rest is blocked by the house. The house's entrance is offstage and is reached from this porch. D. S. is a woodshed attached to Mrs. Potts' house by the roof. This woodshed (separated from the yard by a trellis-like wall) extends to the extreme D. S. edge of the set. The space between the woodshed and house forms a narrow passageway leading to the rest of Mrs. Potts' property. A rough wooden door leads from the yard into this passageway. This is referred to as the "shed door." When "the porch" is referred to, this means Flo's porch, Mrs. Potts' porch is always specifically designated as such.

When the curtain goes up it is early morning and the stage is empty. It is late summer, Labor Day, and autumn has just begun to edge the green landscape with a rim of brown. The scene has the color of luscious fruit just be-

6

ginning to ripen. Dew is still on the countryside and mist rises from the earth in the distance. Far off, the whistle of a train is heard coming to town. It is a happy promising sound. A factory whistle blows, a dog barks and a moment later Mrs. Potts appears on her porch. She stops, looks off L., motions to someone to follow her, and then goes down the steps to the door of the shed as Hal Carter appears on the porch carrying a trash barrel on his shoulder. Hal is an exceedingly handsome youth, dressed in T-shirt, dungarees and cowboy boots. Mrs. Potts opens the shed door and disappears inside. Hal looks around him for a moment. Then he goes down the steps to the tree stump, puts his right foot up on the stump, takes the barrel off his shoulder and rests it on his knee while he takes a breath. Mrs. Potts returns from the shed with a leaf rake which she leans against the U. S. corner of the shed as she speaks.

MRS. POTTS. (L. of Hal.) You just had a big breakfast. Wouldn't you like to rest a while before you start to work?
HAL. Work's good for my digestion, Mam. (He looks away, concerned.)
MRS. POTTS. Now, stop being embarrassed because you asked for breakfast. That's nothing.
HAL. I never done it before.
MRS. POTTS. What's the difference? You probably never had cherry pie for breakfast before either!
HAL. That's right, Mam, I didn't. (Mrs. Potts starts out L.—D. S. of shed. Hal puts the barrel on his shoulder and starts after her. She stops and turns to him.)
MRS. POTTS. You're going to be awfully hot working in that jacket.
HAL. My shirt's awful dirty, Mam.
MRS. POTTS. I'll wash it while you're burning the trash.
HAL. I sure would like to feel clean. (He looks around, worried.) Would anybody object?
MRS. POTTS. Of course not! You're a man! What's the difference? (She laughs and goes off D. S. L., Hal following her. Millie Owens enters the porch from the kitchen of the house at R. She is a girl of sixteen and wears a denim shirt, dungarees and sneakers.

7

A bicycle bell rings off U. L. *Millie hears it and moves more quickly to the front steps, grabbing her cap from a nail by the kitchen door. She sits on the* R. *side of the steps and gets a cigarette and matches out of her hiding place by the step and lights up as Bomber, a newsboy, rides in from alley* U. L., *throws a paper on Mrs. Potts' porch, parks his bike* U. R. *of the alley gate and taking a paper with him crosses down to the* C. *of the lawn, looking up at Madge Owens' window. Bomber slams the paper down on the porch, trying to attract attention. He succeeds.*)

MILLIE. Hey, Crazy, you want to knock the house down?

BOMBER. I don't hear you.

MILLIE. If you ever break a window you'll hear me!

BOMBER. (*Crosses* D. *to* C.) Go back to bed and tell your pretty sister to come out. It's no fun lookin' at you! (*Millie ignores him. Bomber crosses to steps, right foot up.*) I'm talkin' to you, Goonface!

MILLIE. (*Jumping up and poising herself for a fight. Bomber jumps back just out of reach.*) You ornery bastard, take that back!

BOMBER. Listen to her! She cusses just like a man!

MILLIE. (*Goes after him with doubled fists.*) I'll kill you, you ornery bastard! I'll kill you! (*Bomber ducks the first blow which is aimed at his head and takes the rest on his arms as he jeers.*)

BOMBER. Lookit Mrs. Tar-zan! Lookit Mrs. Tar-zan!

MADGE. (*Comes on to porch from front door. She is eighteen and very beautiful. She is drying her hair with a towel. She sits on the porch corner.*) Who's making all this noise? (*Bomber looks up seeing Madge and the fight stops.*)

BOMBER. (*Crosses to Madge.*) Hi, Madge!

MADGE. Hi, Bomber.

BOMBER. I hope I didn't wake you, Madge, or bother you or anything. (*Millie crosses* U. *to paper which Bomber threw on porch.*)

MADGE. Of course not.

BOMBER. Hey, Madge, a bunch of us guys are chippin' in on a hot-rod—radio and everything. I get it every Friday night. (*Millie crosses* D., *sits on chair in* C. *of yard, opens paper as she crosses.*)

MADGE. I'm not one of those girls that jump in a hot-rod every time you boys turn a corner and honk.

MILLIE. Alan Seymour sends her flowers every time they go out.

8

BOMBER. (*To Madge.*) I can't send you flowers, Baby—but I can send you!

MILLIE. Listen to him braggin'.

BOMBER. (*Squat at Madge's L. on step.*) Lemme pick you up some night after Seymour brings you home.

MADGE. That wouldn't be fair to Alan, would it? We go steady.

MILLIE. (*To Bomber.*) Don't you know what "steady" means, stupid?

BOMBER. (*Ignoring Millie.*) I seen you riding around in his Cadillac like you was a Duchess. (*He turns away to* C. *Hal enters from* D. L. *and gets rake from the shed.*) Why do good looking girls have to be so stuck on themselves?

MADGE. (*Jumps up, furious.*) I'm not stuck on myself! You take that back, Bomber Gutzel!

BOMBER. (*Turning back to her.*) Lemme pick you up some night!

MADGE. (*Walks* U. *to kitchen door, disgusted.*) Bomber!

BOMBER. (*Following her.*) We'll get some cans of beer ——

MILLIE. Why don't you leave her alone! (*Madge crosses* D. *on porch to front door, Bomber following. Hal, growing interested, leans rake against trellis and ambles to* C.)

BOMBER. (*Grabbing Madge's arm.*) Aw, c'mon, Madge! Give a guy a break!

HAL. (*To Bomber. Crosses to* C.) On your way, lover boy!

BOMBER. (*Crosses* L. *to meet Hal.*) Who're you?

HAL. (*Smiling.*) What's that matter? I'm bigger'n you are. (*Bomber realizes this is true, and after a moment of indecision, starts off hurriedly.*)

MILLIE. (*Calling after Bomber.*) Go peddle your papers! Ok— ok—ok—ok—ok! (*Bomber crosses* U. C. *to bicycle and quickly rides off* R. *alley. Hal watches him go then turns to Millie. Madge sits on porch, feet on* C. *of top step.*)

HAL. Hey, kid, got a smoke?

MILLIE. (*Taking out cigarette.*) You workin' for Mrs. Potts?

HAL. (*Feeling pockets for matches.*) Yeah, I'm doin' a few odd jobs around the yard.

MILLIE. (*Hands him matches.*) She give you breakfast?

HAL. (*Embarrassed about it.*) Yah.

MADGE. (*Disapprovingly.*) Millie!

HAL. (*Turning to Madge—quick smile.*) Hi.

MADGE. (*Returning smile.*) Hi.

9

HAL. (*Turning* U. L., *to himself.*) Hi hi!

FLO. (*Comes out of front door onto porch, carrying an evening dress on which she works during the following scene and a sewing basket and Madge's manicure set. She crosses to armchair and puts dress on it. Puts sewing basket on floor next to chair. Returns to* C. *and gives Madge manicure set, who places it on floor where she sits. Then she sees Hal. As Flo enters, Millie puts out her cigarette on her heel.*) Young man, this is my house and these are my daughters.

HAL. (*Turns and crosses to* C. *as Flo speaks.*) They are?

FLO. (*She nods.*) Is there something you want?

HAL. Just loafin', Mam.

FLO. This is a busy day for us. You better run along.

HAL. It's your house, lady. (*Crosses* L. *to shed, turns to Flo.*) You're their *mother*? (*Flo nods. Hal shakes his head in admiration and walks off to Mrs. Potts' yard through door of shed, taking rake with him which leans against trellis.*)

FLO. (*When Hal is off she crosses* D. L.) Has Helen Potts taken in another tramp?

MADGE. I don't see why he's a tramp just because Mrs. Potts gave him breakfast.

FLO. I'm going to speak to her about the way she takes in every Tom, Dick and Harry!

MADGE. He wasn't doing any harm.

FLO. I bet he'd like to. (*Crosses to armchair on porch and picks up dress.*) Have you called Alan this morning?

MADGE. No, I haven't had time.

MILLIE. He's coming by pretty soon to take us swimming.

FLO. (*To Madge.*) Tell him they're expecting a big crowd at the park this evening, so he'd better use his father's influence at the City Hall to reserve a table. Oh, and tell him to get one down by the river, close to a Dutch oven.

MADGE. He'll think I'm being bossy.

FLO. Alan doesn't mind if a woman's bossy. (*Sits in armchair and starts work on dress. A train whistle in the distance off* L.)

MADGE. Whenever I hear that train coming into town, I always get a feeling of excitement . . . in here. (*Hugging her stomach.*)

MILLIE. Whenever I hear it, I tell myself some day I'm going to get on that train and I'm going to go to New York.

FLO. That train only goes as far as Tulsa.

MILLIE. Well, in Tulsa I could catch another train.

MADGE. I always wonder, maybe some wonderful person is getting off here, just by accident, and he'll come into the dime store for something and see me behind the counter, and he'll study me very strangely and then decide I'm just the person they're looking for in Washington to carry on an important job in the Espionage Department. (*She puts towel over face below eyes.*) Or maybe he wants me for some great medical experiment!

FLO. Those things don't happen in dime stores. (*Millie rustles her paper.*) Madge —— (*She wants to get rid of Millie.*) Millie, would you take the milk in, please? (*Millie lowers paper, looks at her mother, rises slowly and crosses* U.)

MILLIE. (*As she exits into kitchen with milk.*) Awwww . . . (*Madge turns away* D. R. *drying hair.*)

FLO. (*After a moment.*) Did you and Alan have a good time on your date last night?

MADGE. Uh-huh.

FLO. What'd you do? (*She continues to work on dress.*)

MADGE. (*Trying to avoid the cross questioning.*) We went over to his house and played some of his classical records.

FLO. (*After a pause.*) Then what'd you do?

MADGE. Drove over to Cherryvale and had some barbecue.

FLO. (*A hard question to ask.*) Madge, does Alan ever . . . make love?

MADGE. When we drive over to Cherryvale we always park the car by the river and get real romantic.

FLO. Do you let him kiss you? After all, you've been going together all summer.

MADGE. Of course I let him.

FLO. Does he ever want to go beyond kissing?

MADGE. (*Embarrassed.*) Mom!

FLO. I'm your mother, for heaven's sake! These things have to be talked about. Does he?

MADGE. Well . . . yes.

FLO. Does Alan get mad if you . . . won't?

MADGE. No.

FLO. (*To herself, puzzled.*) He doesn't . . .

MADGE. He doesn't get *mad*.

FLO. Do *you* like it when he kisses you?

MADGE. Yes.

11

FLO. You don't sound very enthusiastic.

MADGE. What do you expect me to do—pass out every time Alan puts his arm around me?

FLO. No, you don't have to pass out. But it seems to me you could at least ——

MADGE. (*Turning to her.*) What?

FLO. (*She rises.*) Hold this dress up in front of you. (*Madge rises, holds dress. Flo sits* U. L. *of her in beach chair and continues work.*) Madge, it'd be awfully nice to be married to Alan. You'd have charge accounts at all the stores—automobiles—trips. You'd be invited by all his friends to parties in their homes and at the country club.

MADGE. (*Uncomfortably.*) Mom, I don't feel right with those people.

FLO. What do you mean? You're just as good as they are. My father was in the State Legislature and my mother's family was one ——

MADGE. (*She gives dress to Flo and crosses* L. *to* C.) I know, Mom, but all of Alan's friends talk about colleges and trips to Europe. I feel left out.

FLO. You've just got to get over those feelings. Now, Alan will be going back to school in a few weeks. There won't be many more opportunities like the picnic tonight. You better get busy.

MADGE. Busy what?

FLO. Madge, a pretty girl doesn't have long—just a few years when she's the equal of kings and can walk out of a shanty like this and live in a palace with a doting husband who'll spend his life making her happy.

MADGE. (*Turning away.*) I suppose, but ——

FLO. Because once, *once* she was young and pretty. If she loses that chance, she might just as well throw all her prettiness away.

MADGE. I'm only eighteen.

FLO. And next summer you'll be nineteen, and then twenty, and then twenty-one, and then forty. (*Crossing with dress to Madge who holds it against her again. Flo squats in front of her. Millie enters from front door with sketch pad and charcoal, looks at new dress then sits on* R. *edge of steps.*)

MILLIE. Everyone around here gets to dress up and go places except me. (*Looking off* R. *sketching.*)

12

MADGE. Alan said he'd try to find you a date for the picnic tonight.

MILLIE. I don't want Alan asking any of these crazy boys in town to take me anywhere.

MADGE. Beggars can't be choosers!

MILLIE. You shut up.

FLO. (*Pinning up hem.*) Madge, that was mean. There'll be dancing at the pavilion tonight. Millie should have a date, too. (*She moves* D. L. *a bit and looks at hem line.*)

MADGE. If she wants a date, why doesn't she dress up and act decent?

MILLIE. 'Cause I'm gonna dress and act the way I want to, and if you don't like it you know what you can do!

MADGE. Always complaining because she doesn't have any friends, but she smells so bad people don't want to be near her! (*Flo covers Madge's mouth. Madge gives dress to Flo and picks up her towel.*)

FLO. Madge!

MILLIE. La-de-da! Madge is the pretty one—but she's so dumb they almost had to burn the schoolhouse down to get her out of it!

MADGE. That's not so!

MILLIE. Oh, isn't it? You never would have graduated if it hadn't been for Jumpin' Jeeter.

FLO. (*Crosses to the steps.*) Who's Jumpin' Jeeter?

MILLIE. Teaches history. Kids call him Jumpin' Jeeter 'cause the pretty girls in his classes make him so jumpy. He was flunking Madge till she went in his room and cried: (*An imitation.*) "I just don't know what I'll do if I don't pass history!"

MADGE. Mom, she's making that up.

MILLIE. Like fun I am! You couldn't even pass Miss Sydney's course in shorthand and you have to work in the dime store!

FLO. Millie!

MADGE. You *are* a goon!

MILLIE. Madge, you slut! (*She starts for Madge who shrieks and runs around stump to kitchen porch. Millie follows to porch.*) You take that back or I'll kill you!

FLO. Millie! Madge! (*She puts dress on porch armchair and runs* u. s. *after girls.*) Girls! Girls! Stop it! What will the neighbors say! (*Millie grabs Madge's hair and pulls it. Madge swats Millie with towel. Millie lets her go. Madge crosses to shed door.*)

13

MILLIE. Nobody's gonna call me a goon and get by with it!

FLO. You called her worse names!

MILLIE. It doesn't hurt what names I call her! She's pretty, names don't bother her at all! (*She storms off porch through front door, near tears.*)

FLO. Poor Millie! (*Crosses* D. *to armchair and picks up dress.*)

MADGE. (*Crosses* R. *to below* C. *chair in yard.*) That's all I hear —"poor Millie," and poor Millie won herself a scholarship for four whole years of college!

FLO. A girl like Millie can need confidence in other ways.

MADGE. Mom?

FLO. Yes?

MADGE. Do you love Millie more than me?

FLO. Of course not!

MADGE. Why do you act as if you did?

FLO. (*Crosses to* L. *of Madge—sits on stump, takes Madge's hands.*) Madge! Madge, listen to me! You were the first born. Your father thought the sun rose and set in you. He used to carry you on his shoulder for the neighborhood to see. But when Millie came things were different.

MADGE. How?

FLO. They were just . . . different. Your father wasn't home much of the time then. He'd found . . . other things. The night Millie was born he was with a bunch of his wild friends at the road house.

MADGE. Was he sorry?

FLO. Yes. He was always sorry. And I always forgave him. (*Crosses to* R. C.) Our life was a succession of fights and endearments.

MADGE. Anyway, you loved him.

FLO. What if I did? It takes a lot more than love to keep people happy. (*She looks at Madge for a moment and then crosses to* U. *of Madge and fluffs her hair to help it dry.*)

MADGE. Mom . . .

FLO. Yes?

MADGE. What good is it to be pretty?

FLO. (*Looks at Madge—puzzled.*) Well . . . pretty things are rare in this life.

MADGE. But what good are they?

FLO. Well . . . pretty things . . . like flowers and sunsets and rubies . . . (*She tries to turn Madge's face to her. Madge pulls away.*) and pretty girls, too . . . they're like billboards telling us that life is good.

MADGE. But where do I come in?

FLO. (*At her R.*) What do you mean?

MADGE. Maybe I get tired being looked at.

FLO. Madge! Don't talk so selfish!

MADGE. I don't care if I am selfish. It's no good just to be pretty. It's no good!

HAL. (*Comes in from Mrs. Potts' yard D. L., jacket in hand.*) Mam, is it all right if I start a fire?

FLO. (*Not paying attention, still concerned about Madge.*) What? (*She looks up, sees that Hal is bare chested. She steps to L. of Madge shielding Hal from view.*)

HAL. The nice lady said it's a hot enough day already and maybe you'd object. How about it, Mam—mind a little fire? (*Madge manages a look past Flo at Hal.*)

FLO. (*She is cold towards him.*) No, I don't mind.

HAL. (*Hangs his jacket on shed door, closes door.*) I didn't think you would. (*He is suddenly conscious of his bare chest. He covers his chest modestly with his hands and walks off D. L.*)

FLO. (*Crosses to U. L. of stump, looking after Hal.*) He's got no shame! He just moves right in whether you want him to or not!

MADGE. I knew you wouldn't like him when I first saw him.

FLO. Do you?

MADGE. I don't like him or dislike him. I just wonder what he's like.

FLO. I *know* what he's like. (*Rosemary Sydney comes out of front door of the house, wearing a dressing gown and carrying a jar of face cream and a hand mirror.*)

ROSEMARY. Anyone mind if an old maid schoolteacher joins their company?

FLO. 'Morning, Rosemary. (*Crosses R. to armchair.*)

ROSEMARY. Mail come yet? (*Madge crosses to R. edge of steps, sits on porch and picks up manicure set.*)

FLO. No mail today. It's Labor Day. (*Flo picks up dress and crosses to chair C. in yard during next speech.*)

ROSEMARY. I forgot. I thought I might be gettin' a letter from that man I met at the high school picnic last spring. (*A bawdy laugh. She sits on porch corner, starts to cream face.*) Been wantin' to marry me ever since. A nice fellow and a peck of fun, but I don't have time for any of 'em when they start gettin' serious on me.

FLO. You schoolteachers are mighty independent! (*Millie wanders onto porch from kitchen, reading a book. She sits on porch edge at* R. C.)

ROSEMARY. Shoot! I lived this long without a man. (*Flo sits in chair* C.) I don't see what's to keep me from getting *on* without one.

FLO. What about Howard?

ROSEMARY. Howard's just a friend-boy . . . not a boy-friend. (*Madge and Millie look at her. Rosemary sniffs the air.*) I smell smoke. (*Rises, looks* L.)

FLO. Helen Potts is having her leaves burned. Smells kind of good, don't you think?

ROSEMARY. (*Seeing Hal offstage* L. *Crosses* L. *to* L. *of stump.*) Who's the young man?

FLO. Just another no-good Helen Potts took in.

ROSEMARY. (*Very concerned.*) Mrs. Owens, he's working over there naked as an Indian. I don't think that's right in the presence of ladies. (*Millie jumps up and runs to far* D. L.)

FLO. Millie! Come back here!

MILLIE. (*Crosses* R. *to steps.*) Gee whiz! I go swimming every day and the boys don't have on half as much as he does now.

FLO. Swimming's different!

MILLIE. Madge ——

MADGE. What?

MILLIE. Can I use your manicure set, just for kicks?

MADGE. If you promise not to get it messy. (*Millie sits* L. *of Madge on steps—Madge gives her manicure set. Millie proceeds to put nail polish on.*)

FLO. Look at the way he's showing off!

ROSEMARY. Who does he think is interested? (*And she looks off at him. Madge and Millie are doubled up with laughter.*)

FLO. (*To Rosemary.*) What's that you're rubbing in?

ROSEMARY. Ponsella Three-Way Tissue Cream. Makes a good base for your makeup.

FLO. There was an article in *The Readers' Digest* about some woman who got skin poisoning from using all those face creams.

ROSEMARY. Harriett Bristol . . . she's the American History

teacher . . . she got ahold of some of that beauty clay last winter and it darn near took her skin off. All we girls thought she had leprosy! (*She looks off at Hal, then turns away again.*)

MILLIE. Madge, how do you do your right hand?

MADGE. If you were nice to people, maybe people would do something nice for *you.*

ROSEMARY. (*Crosses to* c.) You got a beau, Millie?

MILLIE. No!

ROSEMARY. You can't kid me! Girls don't paint their fingernails without a reason!

FLO. (*Rises.*) Madge, will you try this dress on now, dear? (*Mrs. Potts enters from* D. L. *and crosses to* D. *of stump. Hal enters behind her carrying a large basket of clothes.*)

MRS. POTTS. Flo!

FLO. (*Calling back, a noise like an owl. She hands dress to Madge who exits by front door.*) Hoooo?

MRS. POTTS. Are you going to be using the clothesline this morning?

FLO. No. (*Mrs. Potts turns, signals to Hal and starts off* D. L.)

HAL. (*To Rosemary.*) Hi.

ROSEMARY. (*Surprised, self-conscious.*) How d'ya do? (*Hal starts out* D. L.)

VOICE. (*Offstage* L. *from Mrs. Potts' house.*) Helen! Helen!

MRS. POTTS. (*Stops.*) I'm hanging out the clothes, Mama. I'll be right back. (*She and Hal exit* D. L. *Millie starts sketching again.*)

FLO. (*To Rosemary—crosses to chair* c.) Poor Helen! She told me sometimes she has to get up *three* times a night to take her mother to the bathroom. (*Sits.*)

ROSEMARY. Why doesn't she put her in an Old Ladies' Home?

FLO. None of 'em will take her. She's too mean.

ROSEMARY. She must be mean . . . if that story you told me is true.

FLO. It is true! Helen and the Potts boy ran off and got married. Helen's mother caught her that very day and had the marriage annulled! (*The sound of an approaching car is heard off* R.)

ROSEMARY. She's Mrs. Potts in name only.

FLO. Sometimes I think she keeps the boy's name just to defy the old lady. (*The car stops and the door slams. Rosemary crosses to porch corner.*)

MILLIE. (*Putting down her book.*) Hi, Alan! (*Jumps up, starts to kitchen door.*) Oh, boy! I'm gonna get my suit!

FLO. (*Calling after Millie.*) See if Madge is decent. (*Alan enters* D. R. *in front of Flo's house. Millie exits into kitchen.*) Good morning, Alan!

ALAN. (*To* R. *of steps.*) 'Morning, Mrs. Owens . . . Miss Sydney.

ROSEMARY. Hello. (*She sits on porch corner. Mrs. Potts enters from* D. L. *hurriedly.*)

MRS. POTTS. Hello, Alan.

ALAN. Hello.

MRS. POTTS. Have you girls seen the handsome young man I've got working for me? (*Sits on stump.*)

ROSEMARY. (*Scoffiingly.*) Handsome!

FLO. Helen Potts, I wish you'd stop taking in all sorts of riff-raff! (*Alan crosses* U. *and sits on beach chair.*)

MRS. POTTS. He isn't riff-raff. He's been to several colleges.

FLO. Colleges—and he begs for breakfast!

MRS. POTTS. He's working for his breakfast! Alan, he said he knew you at the University. I told him you might be by.

ALAN. Who? (*Millie dashes on through kitchen door with bathing suit rolled up in towel.*)

MILLIE. (*Crosses* D. *to corner of house.*) Hey, Alan. We going swimming?

ALAN. (*Rising.*) You bet.

FLO. Alan, why don't you go up and see Madge? Just call from the bottom of the stairs.

ALAN. Okay. (*Goes out front door, calling.*) Hey, Delilah! (*Millie puts towel on porch* U. *of chair* C. *and follows Alan.*)

FLO. Millie! (*Millie turns, caught just inside front door. Flo signals for her to come out. Millie does so, pulling her hat over her face disgustedly—then crosses* D., *sits step facing* R.—*picks up book and begins to read.*)

ROSEMARY. Do you think Alan's going to marry Madge?

FLO. I hadn't thought much about it. (*Millie looks at Flo from under her cap visor. Rosemary looks at Millie.*)

MRS. POTTS. (*After a moment.*) It's so hot and still this time of year. When it gets this way I'd welcome a good cyclone . . . even if it blew everything away.

FLO. Hm . . . not me.

MRS. POTTS. (*Looking off at Hal.*) Look at him lift that wash tub as if it was so much tissue paper!

VOICE. (*Offstage from Mrs. Potts' house.*) Helen! Helen!

MRS. POTTS. I'm visiting Flo, Mama. You don't need me.

FLO. What did you feed him?

MRS. POTTS. Biscuits.

FLO. Helen Potts—you went to all that trouble?

MRS. POTTS. He was *so* hungry. I gave him ham and eggs and all the hot coffee he could drink. Then he saw a piece of cherry pie in the icebox and he wanted that, too!

ROSEMARY. (*Laughs bawdily.*) Sounds to me like Mrs. Potts has herself a new boy friend!

MRS. POTTS. (*Gets up, injured.*) I don't think that's very funny.

ROSEMARY. (*Rises—crosses to R. of C. chair.*) Shoot, Mrs. Potts, I'm just a tease.

MRS. POTTS. (*Still touchy.*) I could sit on my own porch, but I hate for the neighbors to see me there all alone. I like to sit over here where there's young people coming and going. (*Madge and Alan come out together, Madge in her new dress. They march out hand in hand in a mock ceremony as though they were going down the aisle and stand on top step, Madge at R.*)

ROSEMARY. (*Crosses to Mrs. Potts.*) Mrs. Potts, if I said anything to offend you ——

FLO. (*Sees Madge and Alan, signals Rosemary to be quiet, points to Madge and Alan.*) Look! Bride and groom! (*To Madge.*) How does it feel, Madge? (*Laughs at her unconscious joke.*) I mean the dress? (*Rosemary crosses to U. L. of stump.*)

MADGE. (*Crossing to her mother, stands facing upstage.*) I love it, Mom, except it's a little tight right back here.

MRS. POTTS. Isn't Madge the pretty one!

ALAN. (*Squats L. of Millie.*) What are you reading, Millie?

MILLIE. (*Turns to him, holding book open for him to see.*) The Ballad of the Sad Cafe. It's wonderful! (*Alan looks at book with Millie.*)

ROSEMARY. (*Shocked.*) Good Lord, Mrs. Owens, you let your daughter read filthy books like that?

FLO. (*Worried.*) Filthy?

ROSEMARY. Everyone in it is some sort of degenerate!

MILLIE. That's not so!

ROSEMARY. It was banned from the library!

19

MRS. POTTS. I don't read much.

FLO. (*Crosses to Millie.*) Millie, give me that book! (*Alan rises. Millie holds onto book tightly.*)

MILLIE. (*Tenaciously.*) No! (*Flo pulls book away from Millie.*)

ALAN. Mrs. Owens, that book is on the reading list at college.

FLO. What's a person to believe? (*Millie takes the book from Flo.*)

ROSEMARY. Well, those college professors don't have any morals! (*Millie and Alan shake hands.*)

FLO. (*Crosses to C. chair—sits.*) Where Millie comes by her tastes, I'll never know.

MADGE. (*As Flo inspects her dress.*) Some of the pictures she has over her bed scare me.

MILLIE. Those pictures are by Picasso, and he's a great artist.

MADGE. A woman with seven eyes. Very pretty.

MILLIE. (*Delivering her ultimatum.*) Pictures don't have to be pretty! (*A sudden explosion from Mrs. Potts' backyard off L. Millie crosses to L. of steps. Alan crosses to C. Flo, Mrs. Potts rise. Rosemary near shed door.*)

FLO. Helen!

MRS. POTTS. I'll go see what it is.

FLO. (*Holding her.*) Stay here! He must have had a gun!

VOICE. (*Offstage from Mrs. Potts' house.*) Helen! Helen!

FLO. (*Still holding Mrs. Potts' arm.*) Don't go over there, Helen! Your mother's old. She has to go soon anyway! (*Mrs. Potts breaks away and runs off D. L.*)

MRS. POTTS. (*Off L.*) What happened out here, young man?

HAL. (*Off L.*) Gee, I don't know, Mam, I just lit this stuff and the whole thing went up.

ALAN. (*As he looks off L.*) Say, that guy looks like —— No, it couldn't be.

ROSEMARY. Isn't that a shame? She'll have to do her whole wash over again.

MRS. POTTS. (*Off L.*) Well, was that bottle in it?

HAL. (*Off L.*) Yeah, I geuss so. (*Mrs. Potts enters from D. L. Flo and the others look at her expectantly.*)

MRS. POTTS. I was a bad girl.

FLO. What *is* it, Helen?

MRS. POTTS. I threw a new bottle of cleaning fluid into the trash this morning.

20

FLO. (*Patting her affectionately.*) Helen Potts, you're the limit! (*She turns, crosses* R. *to front door.*) Come on, Madge, let's finish that dress. (*Madge goes in front door, Rosemary starts to front door, Mrs. Potts beckons to Millie who crosses* L. *toward her.*)

ROSEMARY. Good Lord, I've got to be getting dressed. (*She exits through front door.*)

MRS. POTTS. Millie, come help me. The young man ran into the clothesline trying to get away. (*She and Millie exit* D. L.)

FLO. Alan, Madge will be right down. Would you wait down here? (*Alan dashes to porch, holds front door as Flo goes in.*)

ALAN. Oh, sure.

MRS. POTTS. (*Off* L.) You go ahead, young man. We'll take care of this.

HAL. (*Off* L.) Gee, I'm awful sorry, Mam. I didn't mean to ——

MRS. POTTS. (*Off* L.) That's all right. Millie will help me. (*Hal backs on from* D. L. *during this and Alan, hearing the voice, turns and stares at Hal unbelievingly but finally he is convinced.*)

ALAN. (*With a roar.*) It is!

HAL. (*Turns and, also with a roar.*) Kid! (*He leaps up to* C. *lawn where Alan meets him and they clasp hands in an enthusiastic shake.*) The lady said you'd be around!

ALAN. Hal Carter!

HAL. I was comin' to see you!

ALAN. (*Suddenly.*) How's the old outboard motor?

HAL. You wanta ride?

ALAN. All gassed up? (*Hal makes the sound of a motor, then nods to Alan, who pantomimes winding starting rope around Hal's head, pulls rope, Hal makes noise of motor starting, Alan jumps up, throws legs around Hal's waist, grabs Hal's nose with one hand, steering him like an outboard motor down onto the level as he yells:*) Ahoy, Brothers, who's Winkin', Blinkin' and Stinkin'! (*He steers Hal in circles. They turn rapidly three times and then Hal dumps Alan to his feet at his* R. *They are both roaring with laughter. Alan flops down on the steps, Hal crosses to* D. L. *of stump.*)

HAL. That used to wake up the whole damn fraternity!

ALAN. The last time I saw you, you were on your way to Hollywood to become a movie hero.

HAL. Oh, that!

21

ALAN. What do you mean "oh, that"! Isn't that what I loaned you a hundred bucks for?

HAL. Sure, Seymour.

ALAN. (*Crosses* L. *to* C.) Well, what happened?

HAL. Things just didn't work out, that's all.

ALAN. I tried to warn you, Hal. Every year some talent scout promised screen tests to all the big athletes.

HAL. (*Puts* L. *foot on stump.*) Oh, I got the test okay! I was about to have a big career. They were gonna call me Brush Carter. How d'ya like that?

ALAN. Yeah?

HAL. Yah! They took a lotta pictures of me with my shirt off. Real rugged! (*He takes a* Warner Bros. *pose of a he-man: clasps hands behind him, with straight arms, looks over left shoulder. As he breaks it they both laugh.*) Then they dressed me up like the Foreign Legion.

ALAN. No kidding?

HAL. Then they put me in a pair of tights—those pants that fit you down here like a glove—(*Runs his hands down his legs to show, then jumps up on the stump.*) and they gave me a big hat with a plume, (*Pantomimes putting on the hat.*) and had me poking at things with swords. (*He gets into duelling position, leaps off stump to right, parries, lunges, withdraws, wipes blood off blade.*) Touche, mug! (*Sheaths his sword with a smack, turns and enjoying the memory of it immensely he crosses to stump, puts foot on stump, facing* L., *speaking as he crosses.*) It was real crazy!

ALAN. (*Crosses to Hal.*) Did they give you any lines to read?

HAL. Yah, that part went okay. It was my teeth.

ALAN. Your teeth?

HAL. Yah! Out there, you gotta have a certain kind of teeth or they can't use you. Don't ask me why. (*Foot down off stump, turn to Alan.*) This babe said they'd have to pull all my teeth and give me new ones, so naturally ——

ALAN. Wait a minute. What babe?

HAL. The babe that got me the screen test. She wasn't a babe exactly. She was kinda beat up—but not bad.

ALAN. Uh-huh. (*Alan crosses to steps—Hal sits on stump, embarrassed, leans far* L., *pulls a blade of grass.*) What are you doing here?

HAL. I came to see you.

ALAN. Yeah? Why?

HAL. Well, you see, after Hollywood I took a job on a ranch in Nevada. Seymour, you'da been proud of me. In bed every night at ten, (*Stretches.*) up every morning at six. No liquor—no babes. I saved up two hundred bucks!

ALAN. Oh, you came to pay me back.

HAL. Well, Seymour, I was gonna—but I got rolled. (*He rises, turns chair to face* D. R. *in his embarrassment.*)

ALAN. Rolled? You?

HAL. Yeah, and by two babes. See —— (*He crosses* u. c.—*looks* L. *then* R., *sees no one, crosses* D.—*squats on* D. R. *lawn next to Alan, who crossed and sat on porch corner.*) See—I was gonna hitch-hike down to Texas to try my luck. I got as far as Phoenix when two babes pull up in this *big* yellow convertible. And this one babe slams on the brakes and she hollers, "Get in, stud!" So I got in. Seymour, it was crazy. They had a shakerful of martinis right there in the car! (*A screen door slams off* u. L. *and Mrs. Potts appears on her porch followed by Millie. Mrs. Potts carries a large chocolate cake.*)

MRS. POTTS. Oh, you boys talking over old times? Millie helped me ice the cake. (*She crosses to Flo's kitchen door, Millie opens door for her.*)

HAL. (*Crosses* L. *to shed.*) Any more work, Mam?

MRS. POTTS. No. I feel more than paid for the breakfast.

HAL. (*Opens shed door, puts rake inside, closes door.*) S'pose there's any place I could wash up?

MILLIE. We got a shower in the basement. Come on, I'll show you. (*Mrs. Potts exits into kitchen. Hal crosses to* u. c. *lawn.*)

ALAN. (*Crosses to intercept Hal.*) He'll be there in a minute. (*Millie exits into kitchen. Alan turns to Hal.*) Okay, so they had a shakerful of martinis right in the car!

HAL. (*Takes Alan* L. *to Mrs. Potts' railing—leans on railing, Alan at his* R.) And one of these babes was smokin' the weed!

ALAN. (*Crosses* R. *to lawn* c.) Nothing like that ever happens to me! (*Turns.*) Well—go on with the story ——

HAL. (*Embarrassed.*) Seymour, you wouldn't believe it, the things those two babes started doin' to me.

ALAN. Were they good looking?

HAL. What do you care?

ALAN. Makes the story more interesting. Tell me what you did exactly.

HAL. Well, you know me, Seymour. I'm an agreeable guy.

ALAN. Sure.

HAL. So when they took me to this tourist cabin, I said, "Okay, girls, if I gotta pay for the ride ——" Well—(*He shrugs and turns away.*) you know, they musta thought I was King Kong.

ALAN. You mean . . . *both* of them?

HAL. Sure.

ALAN. (*Crosses* R. *to* C. *lawn.*) Golly!

HAL. Then I said, "Okay, girls, the party's over—let's get goin'." Then this dame on the weed, she sticks a gun in my back. She says, "This party's goin' on till *we* say it's over, Buck!" You'da thought she was Humphrey Bogart!

ALAN. What happened?

HAL. Finally I passed out! (*Alan crosses to* C. *steps and sits.*) And when I woke up, the dames were gone and so was my two hundred bucks! (*Crosses* D. R. *to porch corner.*) I went to the police and they wouldn't believe me—they said my story was wishful thinking! How d'ya like *that!* (*Crosses to* U. C. *lawn.*)

ALAN. Mmmm.

HAL. (*Crosses* D. C.) I'm telling you, Seymour, women are gettin' desperate. Well, that did it. (*Sits* C.—*lies down, head* L.) Then I thought, what's a poor bastard like me ever gonna do.

ALAN. You don't sound to me like you'd had such a bad life.

HAL. Then I got thinking of you, Seymour, at school—how *you* always had things under control.

ALAN. Me?

HAL. Yah. Never cut classes . . . understood the lectures . . . (*He sits up.*) took notes! (*Alan laughs.*) What's so funny?

ALAN. The one authentic hero the University had, and he envied me!

HAL. Yah! Big hero, but just between the goal posts. Seymour, you're the only guy in the whole fraternity ever treated me like a human being.

ALAN. I know.

HAL. Those other phonies always watchin' to see if I used the singular instead of the plural.

ALAN. You just imagined that.

HAL. In a pig's eye, I did!

ALAN. Why do you feel you're any worse than everybody else?

HAL. (*Lies down, head* L.) Maybe I'll tell you some day.

ALAN. Your father drinks. So what? It happens in the best of families.

HAL. He died in jail, Seymour, the last time they scraped him up off the sidewalk.

ALAN. Gee, Hal, I'm awfully sorry to hear that.

HAL. The old lady wouldn't even come across with the dough for the funeral. They had to bury him in Pauper's Row.

ALAN. What about the filling station?

HAL. Oh, he left it to me in his will, but the old lady wanted it so bad she was gonna have him declared insane. So I let her have it. Who needs it?

ALAN. Yeah. When did you get into town?

HAL. This morning, on a freight.

ALAN. Why didn't you come to see me right away?

HAL. I didn't want to walk into your palatial mansion lookin' like a bum.

ALAN. That wouldn't have made any difference.

HAL. I wanted to pick up some change and buy a new shirt. I was hoping maybe you and your old man, between you, might fix me up with a job.

ALAN. What kind of a job, Hal?

HAL. What kinda jobs you got?

ALAN. What did you have in mind?

HAL. (*Sits up.*) Oh, something in a nice office where I can wear a tie . . . and have a sweet little secretary . . . and talk over the telephone about enterprises and . . . things. (*Alan walks away to* D. L. *of stump. Hal rises—crosses to* D. C.) I've always had the feeling, if I just had the chance, I could set the whole world on fire.

ALAN. (*Reasonably.*) Maybe you could, Hal. (*Turns to Hal.*) But for the time being you've got to be content to work hard and be patient.

HAL. Yah! That's something I gotta learn. *Patience!* (*Hal turns* D. R. *Mrs. Potts enters from Flo's kitchen.*)

ALAN. Mrs. Potts, Sinclair is hiring new men, aren't they?

MRS. POTTS. Yes, Alan. Carey wants a hundred men for the pipeline.

ALAN. How about the pipeline, Hal?

25

HAL. Great . . . great. (*He shakes hands with Alan. He goes to Mrs. Potts, looks at her, kisses her, then exits into kitchen.*) Where's that shower!

MRS. POTTS. (L. *of bench on porch.*) Isn't he a nice young man? (*Rosemary enters from front door in a brand new outfit, a fall suit and an elaborate hat.*)

ROSEMARY. Is this a private party I'm crashing?

MRS. POTTS. (*Crosses* D. *to above armchair.*) My, you're dressed up!

ROSEMARY. (*To* D. R. *of door.*) 'S my new fall outfit. Got it in Kansas City. Paid $22.50 for the hat.

MRS. POTTS. You school teachers do have nice things. (*Crosses* R. *to beach chair.*)

ROSEMARY. And don't have to ask anybody when we wanta get 'em, either. (*Crosses* L. *to* D. *of door. Flo enters from kitchen with bowl of devilled eggs and a spoon.*)

FLO. Be here for lunch today, Rosemary? (*Crosses* D. *to* U. *of armchair.*)

ROSEMARY. No. There's a welcome home party down at the hotel. Lunch and bridge for the new girls on the faculty. (*Madge enters from kitchen—crosses* D. *to* L. *of bench.*)

MADGE. Mom, can I go swimming?

FLO. Who'll fix lunch? I've got a million things to do.

MADGE. It wouldn't kill Millie if she ever did any cooking.

FLO. No, but it might kill the rest of us. (*She sits in armchair. Now we hear the voices of Irma Kronkite and Christine Schoenwalder, off* U. L., *who are coming by for Rosemary. They think it playful to call from a distance.*)

IRMA. (*Offstage* U. L.) Rosemary! Let's get going, girl! Don't wanta be late! (*As they come into sight in alley* U. L., *Irma turns to Christine. Rosemary crosses* D. *onto top step, facing front, preparing for them.*) You'll love Rosemary Sydney. She's a peck of fun!

ROSEMARY. (*With playful suspiciousness.*) What're you saying about me, Irma Kronkite? (*They run to hug each other like eager sisters who had not met in a decade. Irma crosses* D. *to* C. *Rosemary crosses to her. Christine crosses to* D. L. *lawn.*)

IRMA. Rosemary Sydney!

ROSEMARY. Irma Kronkite! How was your vacation?

26

IRMA. I worked like a slave. But I had fun, too. I don't care if I *never* get that Masters. I'm not going to be a slave *all* my life.

CHRISTINE. (*Shyly.*) She's been telling me about all the wicked times she had in New York—and not at Teachers' College, if I may add. (*Irma crosses* U., *takes Christine's arm and leads her down to* C.)

IRMA. Kid, this is Christine Schoenwalder, taking Mabel Freemont's place in Feminine Hygiene. (*Christine crosses* D. *to Rosemary, they shake hands.*)

ROSEMARY. How do you do, Christine? (*She takes Christine to porch and introduces her to Mrs. Potts. Irma crosses to porch.*)

IRMA. Been a hot summer, Mrs. Owens?

FLO. Terrible.

MRS. POTTS. Delighted to know you, Christine. (*They shake hands.*) Welcome back, Irma.

ROSEMARY. (*Taking Christine to Flo.*) And this is Mrs. Owens, Christine Shoenwalder. (*As Flo and Christine greet each other, Irma crosses to Mrs. Potts, greets her and then turns to Madge. Irma is now left of Mrs. Potts, Christine is above Flo, Rosemary is below front door.*)

IRMA. Are you working now, Madge?

MADGE. Yes.

FLO. (*Hurriedly.*) Yes, Madge took a job downtown this summer —just to keep busy. (*Hal and Millie burst out the kitchen door engaged in a mock fight, Millie punching, Hal blocking. Hal is still bare-chested and the sight of him is a great shock to the ladies. Mrs. Potts crosses to* R. *of Flo.*) Why, when did he ——?

ALAN. (*Crosses to Hal and Millie.*) Hal! Hal! Millie! (*He finally stops the boxing and as he leads Hal down to* L. *of Flo:*) Mrs. Owens, I'd like you to meet a friend of mine—Hal Carter. Hal is a fraternity brother.

MRS. POTTS. (*Nudging Flo.*) See?

FLO. (*Stunned.*) Fraternity brother, really? (*Making the best of it.*) Well, any friend of Alan's is a friend of ours. (*She offers her hand to Hal.*)

HAL. (*As he takes her hand.*) Thanks, Mam. Glad to make your acquaintance.

ALAN. Hal, don't you have a shirt?

MRS. POTTS. I washed it and—it isn't dry yet.

HAL. Yeah, it was all sweaty. (*The ladies react to this and Hal*

27

realizes he has said the wrong thing. He goes to join Millie. Alan crosses L. to Madge.)

ROSEMARY. Girls, we better get a hustle on. *(Rosemary crosses D. to R. of steps. Irma crosses to porch edge above steps. Christine crosses L. and D. to L. of porch corner.)*

CHRISTINE. *(To Irma.)* Tell them about what happened in New York, kid.

IRMA. *(The center of attention.)* I went to the Stork Club!

ROSEMARY. How did *you* get to the Stork Club?

IRMA. See, there was this fellow in my Educational Statistics class . . .

ROSEMARY. I *knew* there was a *man* in it.

IRMA. Now, girl! It was nothing serious. He was just a good sport, that's all. We made a bet that the one who made the lowest grade on the *final* had to take the other to the Stork Club—and *I* lost! *(To Christine and Rosemary.)* Come on. *(As the teachers exit D. L. chattering to each other, Hal beckons to Millie who follows him to back of yard where he shows her a balancing trick: they both face R., he bends his knees, lifts her so she stands on his thighs. He holds her legs below the knee, and with her weight counterbalancing his, he leans back as she leans forward, stretching her arms out as in a dive. Meanwhile:)*

FLO. *(Sits on porch edge, R. of steps.)* I should think they'd smother in all those clothes.

ALAN. *(Who has been talking to Madge.)* Say, Hal, would you like to go swimming?

HAL. Why not?

MRS. POTTS. Flo, let's ask the young man on the picnic. He'd be a date for Millie. *(She crosses U. to L. of bench on porch.)*

FLO. That's right, but—Helen ——

MRS. POTTS. Young man, *(Millie jumps down. Hal moves to R. gate post.)* Flo and I are having a picnic at the park tonight for the young people. You come, too, and be an escort for Millie.

HAL. Picnic?

MRS. POTTS. Uh-huh.

HAL. *(Leans on U. S. kitchen porch post.)* Gee, Mam, I don't think it's right me bargin' in this way.

MRS. POTTS. Nonsense. A picnic's no fun without lots and lots of young people.

ALAN. Hal! *(Hal crosses D. to D. C. lawn. Alan crosses to him,*

leading Madge to his L. *Millie crosses* D. *to* D. S. *kitchen post.*)
I want you to meet Madge.

MADGE. Oh, we've met already. That is, we *saw* each other.

HAL. Yah, we saw each other.

ALAN. (*To Madge.*) Hal notices every beautiful girl. (*He gives Hal a playful kick.*)

MADGE. (*Pretending to protest.*) Alan.

ALAN. Well, you're the most beautiful girl in town, aren't you? (*To Hal.*) The Chamber of Commerce voted her Queen of Neewollah last year.

HAL. What?

MILLIE. (*Crosses* D. *a step.*) Neewollah. Neewollah is Hallowe'en spelled backwards.

MRS. POTTS. Every year they have a big coronation ceremony in Memorial Hall.

MILLIE. Madge had to sit through the whole ceremony till they put a crown on her head.

HAL. (*Impressed.*) Yah?

MADGE. I got awfully tired.

MRS. POTTS. The *Kansas City Star* ran color photographs in their Sunday magazine.

MADGE. Everyone expected me to get real conceited, but I didn't. (*Crosses* D. L. *to shed.*)

HAL. You didn't?

MILLIE. Well, it'd be pretty hard to get conceited about *those* pictures. (*Crosses* D. *to* D. R. *lawn, makes a face.*)

MADGE. The color got blurred and they printed my mouth right in the middle of my forehead.

HAL. (*Sympathetic.*) Gee, that's too bad.

MILLIE. (*Picks up towel.*) Come on —— (*She hits him in the stomach.*) Let's go swimming. I'll race you to the car.

HAL. Isn't your sister goin' with us?

MILLIE. No, Madge has to cook lunch.

HAL. Do you mean *she cooks?*

MILLIE. Sure! Madge cooks and sews and does all those things that women do. Come on. (*She punches him. Hal squats down in position of racing start.*)

HAL. On your mark!

MILLIE. (*Getting into similar position.*) I'm on my mark.

HAL. Get set!

29

MILLIE. I'm set!

HAL. GO! Go—go—go—go! (*He slaps her fanny and she starts running for the gate to alley. He dashes to the porch corner, grabs the porch post and easily jumps the fence dropping in the alley just ahead of Millie who has just gone through the gate. Hal races off ahead of her and she follows yelling after him.*)

MILLIE. Hey, that's no fair! (*Hal and Millie are gone.*)

FLO. (*Rises.*) Alan!

ALAN. (*Crosses to L. of C. chair in yard.*) Yes?

FLO. (*Crosses to C.*) How did a boy like him get into college?

ALAN. On a football scholarship.

FLO. Oh.

ALAN. He made a spectacular record in a little high school down in Arkansas.

FLO. But a fraternity! Don't those boys have more . . . breeding?

ALAN. Maybe, but fraternities like to pledge big athletes—for the publicity. And Hal could have been All-American ——

MRS. POTTS. (*Delighted.*) All-American!

ALAN. —if he'd only studied. (*Puts L. foot on stump.*) But I know what you're thinking, Mrs. Owens.

FLO. How did the other boys feel about him? Was he popular?

ALAN. They didn't like him, Mrs. Owens. They were pretty rough on him. (*Takes foot down.*) When he came around, every man on that campus seemed to bristle. When I first met him I couldn't stand the way he bragged and swaggered and posed all over the place, and then I found out he's done most of the things he says he's done. He's a fabulous character!

FLO. Do you like him now, Alan?

ALAN. Yes. Hal's really a nice guy, believe it or not. We shared the same room till he flunked out. He told me some of the things he was up against as a kid. It was pretty typical.

FLO. Is he wild?

ALAN. Oh . . . not really. He just . . . Mrs. Owens, if you'd like to withdraw your invitation, I'm sure ——

MRS. POTTS. No ——

FLO. Oh, no, Alan—not if you . . . Does he drink?

ALAN. A little. (*Trying to minimize. He crosses to L. of Flo.*) Mrs. Owens, Hal pays attention to me. I'll see he behaves.

FLO. I wouldn't want anything to happen to Millie.

MADGE. Mom, Millie can take care of herself.

FLO. Maybe you're right. Come on, Helen. (*As she and Mrs. Potts go off.*) Oh, dear, why can't things be simple? (*Mrs. Potts exits into kitchen—Flo follows her. Alan crosses to corner of porch.*)

ALAN. Madge, I'm sorry I have to go back to school this fall. It's Dad's idea.

MADGE. (*Crosses to L. of stump.*) I'm sure of that.

ALAN. (*Crosses to below c. chair.*) What? Wasn't Dad nice last night while I was out fixing the drinks?

MADGE. Oh, yes, he's always very nice to me—very polite. He explained how sorry he was you had to go away.

ALAN. Are you sorry?

MADGE. Of course. (*Sits on stump.*) There'll be lots of pretty girls at college.

ALAN. (*Sits on c. chair.*) Honestly, Madge, my entire four years I never found a girl I liked.

MADGE. I don't believe that.

ALAN. It's true. They're all so affected, if you wanted a date with them you had to call them a month in advance.

MADGE. Really?

ALAN. Madge, it's sort of hard for me to say this, but I honestly never believed that a girl like you could care for me.

MADGE. (*Touched.*) Alan . . .

ALAN. I . . . I hope you do care for me, Madge. (*He kisses her. Hal enters D. R., stops when he sees them and puts L. foot on step.*)

HAL. Hey, Seymour . . . (*Madge and Alan break apart abruptly. She crosses to shed. He turns to Hal.*)

ALAN. What's the matter, Hal? Can't you stand to see anyone else kiss a pretty girl?

HAL. What the hell, Seymour . . .

ALAN. Hal, will you watch your language!

MADGE. Alan! It's all right.

HAL. I'm sorry. (*Beckons Alan to him.*)

ALAN. (*Crossing to him.*) What's the trouble? (*Madge walks away to u. L. lawn, sensing that Hal wants to talk privately.*)

HAL. Look, Seymour, I . . . I never been on a picnic.

ALAN. Not even when you were a kid?

HAL. No.

ALAN. Why, that's impossible! Everybody's been on a picnic.

31

HAL. Not me. I wouldn't go on picnics. I was too busy shooting craps or stealing milk bottles.

ALAN. You went on the steak fries in the fraternity, didn't you?

HAL. Yeah, and you know what *they* turned out to be.

ALAN. Well, Mrs. Potts' picnic won't be quite as primitive.

HAL. That's what I mean. I wouldn't know how to behave in front of all these . . . women.

ALAN. Sure you would.

HAL. But, Seymour, these are . . . *nice* women. What if I say the wrong word or what if my stomach growls—or ——

ALAN. You're a psycho! Run along—I'll be there in a minute. (*Hal starts out* D. R. *Alan crosses* U. *to* U. R. *lawn. Hal stops.*)

HAL. Hey, hurry it up, will you? (*He exits* D. R. *Alan stops, looks back at Hal in disgust then crosses to* U. C. *lawn.*)

ALAN. I'll see you tonight, Madge.

MADGE. All right, Alan.

ALAN. (*He takes her hands.*) Madge, after we have supper to-night maybe you and I can get away from the others and take a boat out on the river.

MADGE. All right, Alan.

ALAN. I want to see if you look real in the moonlight.

MADGE. Alan! Don't say that!

ALAN. Why? I don't care if you're real or not. You're the most beautiful thing I ever saw.

MADGE. Just the same, I'm real. (*As Alan starts to kiss her, we hear several blasts of an automobile horn off* R.)

HAL. (*Offstage* R.) Hey, Seymour—get the lead outa your pants! (*Alan goes off, irritated. Madge crosses to* C. *lawn, watches them as they drive away, waving to them.*)

FLO. (*Inside house.*) Madge! Come on in, dear!

MADGE. All right, Mom. (*As she starts in kitchen door, we hear a train whistle in the distance. Madge hears it and leans against* D. S. *kitchen porch post, looking off* D. L. *listening to the whistle.*)

CURTAIN

32

ACT II

It is late afternoon, the same day. The sun is beginning to set and fills the atmosphere with radiant orange. When the curtain goes up, Millie is in the front doorway, holding the screen door open. She has permitted herself to "dress up" and wears a becoming, feminine dress in which she cannot help feeling a little strange. She is quite attractive. Piano music can be heard offstage, somewhere past Mrs. Potts' house, and Millie stands listening to it for a moment. Then she begins to sway to the music and in a moment is dancing a strange, impromptu dance over the porch and yard. The music stops suddenly and Millie's mood is broken. She rushes upstage and calls off L.

MILLIE. Don't quit now, Ernie! (*She cannot hear Ernie's reply.*) Huh? (*Madge enters from kitchen. Millie turns to Madge.*) Ernie's waiting for the rest of the band to practice. They're going to play out at the park tonight.

MADGE. I don't know why you couldn't have helped us in the kitchen.

MILLIE. (*Lightly, giving her version of the sophisticated belle.*) I had to dress for the ball.

MADGE. (*Crosses D.—sits C. chair in yard.*) I had to make the potato salad and stuff the eggs and make three dozen bread-and-butter sandwiches. (*Puts her feet up on stump.*)

MILLIE. (*In a very affected accent. She crosses D. to U. L. of stump.*) I had to bathe . . . and dust my limbs with powder . . . and slip into my frock.

MADGE. Did you clean out the bath tub?

MILLIE. Yes, I cleaned out the bath tub. (*She becomes very self-conscious.*) Madge, how do I look? Now tell me the truth.

MADGE. You look very pretty. I always knew you could.

MILLIE. I feel sorta funny.

33

MADGE. You look wonderful in the dress. You can have it if you want to.

MILLIE. Thanks. (*A pause.*) Madge, how do you talk to boys?

MADGE. (*Takes feet down.*) Why, you just talk, silly.

MILLIE. How d'ya think of things to say?

MADGE. I don't know. You just say whatever comes into your head.

MILLIE. Supposing nothing ever comes into my head?

MADGE. You talked with him all right this morning.

MILLIE. (*Moves close to stump.*) But now I've got a *date* with him, and it's *different!*

MADGE. You're crazy.

MILLIE. (*Crosses to R. of Madge.*) I think he's a big show-off. (*Turns to Madge.*) You should have seen him this morning on the high diving board. He did real graceful swan dives, and a two and a half gainer, and a back flip . . . the kids stood around clapping. He just ate it up.

MADGE. (*Her mind elsewhere.*) I think I'll paint my toenails tonight and wear sandals.

MILLIE. And he was braggin' all afternoon how he used to be a deep-sea diver off Catalina Island.

MADGE. Honest?

MILLIE. And he says he used to make hundreds of dollars doin' parachute jumps out of a balloon. (*She crosses to L. of porch corner.*) Do you believe it?

MADGE. I don't see why not.

MILLIE. You never hear Alan bragging that way.

MADGE. Alan never jumped out of a balloon.

MILLIE. (*Sits on porch corner.*) Madge, I think he's . . . er . . . girl crazy, too.

MADGE. You think every boy you see is something horrible.

MILLIE. Alan took us into the Hi Ho for cokes and there was a gang of girls in the back booth—Juanita Badger and her gang. (*Madge groans at hearing this name.*) When they saw him, they started giggling and tee-heeing and saying all sorts of crazy things. Then Juanita Badger comes up to me and whispers, "I think he's the cutest thing I ever saw." Is he, Madge?

MADGE. (*Not willing to go overboard.*) I wouldn't say he was "the cutest thing I ever *saw*."

MILLIE. Juanita Badger's an old floozy. She sits in the back row

34

at the movie so the boys that come in will see her and sit with her. One time she and Rubberneck Krauss were asked by the management to leave—and they weren't just kissin', either!

MADGE. (*Laughing.*) I never even speak to Juanita Badger.

MILLIE. Madge, do you think he'll like me?

MADGE. If you give him a chance, he will.

MILLIE. I don't really care. I just wonder. (*Turns away, attempting unconcern.*)

MADGE. Why ask me all the questions? You're supposed to be the smart one.

MILLIE. Not when it comes to boys. I'm absolutely ignorant.

FLO. (*Coming out of kitchen to lawn* C.) Now I tell myself I've got two beautiful daughters.

MILLIE. (*Embarrassed.*) Be quiet, Mom!

FLO. (*Crosses* D. *to* U. *of Madge.*) Doesn't Millie look pretty, Madge?

MADGE. When she isn't picking her nose.

FLO. Madge! (*Crosses to* U. *of Millie on porch corner.*) She doesn't want anyone to be pretty but her.

MILLIE. You're just saying I'm pretty because you're my Mom.

FLO. (*Leans down patting her shoulders fondly.*) Does that keep it from being true? Run over and show Helen Potts how nice you look.

MILLIE. (*Crosses to* C. *lawn and announces herself with broad gestures and loud voice.*) Here comes Millie Owens, the great beauty of all times! Be prepared to swoon when you see her! (*She climbs up over the side of Mrs. Potts' porch and disappears.*)

FLO. (*Sits on armchair on porch, leans back, exhausted.*) Whatever possessed me to let Helen Potts ask that young hoodlum to take Millie on the picnic?

MADGE. Hal?

FLO. Yes, Hal, or whatever his name is. He left every towel in the bathroom black as dirt.

MADGE. It won't hurt anyone just to be nice to him.

FLO. Madge, if there's any drinking tonight, I want you to put a stop to it.

MADGE. I'm not going to be a wet blanket.

FLO. (*Changing the subject.*) Well, you'd better start getting dressed, darling. And don't spend the whole evening admiring yourself in the mirror.

35

MADGE. (*Rises, crosses to shed.*) Mom, don't make fun of me.

FLO. (*Crosses to above stump.*) Madge, you shouldn't object to being kidded when it's well meant.

MADGE. It just seems that when I'm looking in the mirror that's the only way I can prove to myself I'm alive.

FLO. Alive?

MADGE. Yes. Lots of the time I wonder if I really exist.

FLO. Madge! You puzzle me. (*Irma enters from D. R. followed by Christine and Rosemary, returning from their afternoon party. They are exhausted and bored.*)

IRMA. We've brought home your wayward girl, Mrs. Owens! (*Madge crosses u. on Mrs. Potts' steps and sits on steps, to avoid the teachers.*)

FLO. (*Turning from Madge.*) Oh, hello. Have a nice party?

IRMA. (*Crosses to C.*) It wasn't a real party. Each girl paid for her own lunch. Then we played bridge all afternoon. (*Christine stands below R. corner of steps. Rosemary crosses u., puts hat and jacket on bench, moves to above armchair on porch.*)

FLO. Food's good at the hotel, isn't it?

IRMA. Not very. (*Christine crosses to lean on arm of beach chair.*) But they serve it to you nice, with honest-to-goodness napkins! Lord, I hate paper napkins! (*Flo sits on stump. Irma scrapes some gravy off her bodice. Silence.*)

CHRISTINE. I had a French-fried pork chop. Mostly fat. What'd you girls have?

ROSEMARY. (*Without enthusiasm.*) I had the stuffed peppers.

IRMA. (*Disquieted.*) I had the Southern fried chicken.

CHRISTINE. Linda Sue Breckenridge had pot roast of veal. Hm! There was only one little hunk of meat in it. All we girls at her table made her call the waiter and complain.

ROSEMARY. (*Moves to D. of front door.*) Well, I should hope so!

IRMA. Good for you! (*There is a pause.*) I thought by now someone might have noticed my new dress.

ROSEMARY. I was going to say something, kid, and then I . . . uh . . .

IRMA. Remember that satin-back crepe I had last year?

ROSEMARY. Don't tell me!

CHRISTINE. My goodness!

IRMA. Mama remodelled it for me while I was at Columbia. I feel like I had a brand-new outfit. (*Furious at the thought.*) But nobody said anything all afternoon!

CHRISTINE. It's so chic.

IRMA. (*This soothes Irma a bit and she beams. But now there is an awkward pause when no one can think of any more to say.*) Well . . . we better run along, Christine. (*She crosses u. to c. lawn.*) Rosemary has a date. (*Turns to Rosemary.*) We'll come by for you in the morning. Don't be late. (*She goes upstage and waits above the alley gate for Christine.*)

CHRISTINE. (*Crossing to L. of Rosemary, putting out her hand.*) Girl, I want to tell you in one afternoon I feel I've known you my whole life.

ROSEMARY. (*Shaking hands.*) I look upon you as an old friend already.

CHRISTINE. (*Overjoyed.*) Aw . . .

ROSEMARY. (*As Christine and Irma go off alley and out u. L.*) Good-bye, girls! (*As teachers disappear, Rosemary sits in armchair.*)

FLO. (*To Rosemary.*) What time's Howard coming by? (*Madge runs across to front door.*)

ROSEMARY. Pretty soon.

MADGE. (*Turning.*) Mom, is there any hot water?

FLO. You'll have to go see, darling.

MADGE. Miss Sydney, would you mind terribly if I used some of your Shalimar?

ROSEMARY. Help yourself!

MADGE. Thanks. (*She goes inside.*)

ROSEMARY. Madge thinks too much about the boys, Mrs. Owens.

FLO. (*Disbelieving.*) Madge? (*The conversation is stopped by the excited entrance of Mrs. Potts from her porch steps. She is followed by Millie who carries another cake. Mrs. Potts crosses to c. lawn. Millie follows to her L. Flo crosses to Millie, L.*)

MRS. POTTS. It's a *miracle*, that's what it is! I never knew Millie could look so pretty. It's just like a movie I saw once with Betty Grable . . . or was it Lana Turner? Anyway, she played the part of a secretary to some very important business man. She wore glasses and did her hair real plain and men didn't pay any notice to her at all. Then one day she took off her glasses and her boss wanted to marry her right away! Now I tell Millie—all the boys are going to fall in love with her!

ROSEMARY. Millie have a date tonight?

FLO. Yes, I'm sorry to say.

MRS. POTTS. Why, Flo!

ROSEMARY. Who is he, Millie? Tell your Aunt Rosemary.

MILLIE. Hal.

ROSEMARY. Who?

FLO. The young man over at Helen's turned out to be a friend of Alan's.

ROSEMARY. Oh, *him!* (*Millie exits into kitchen carrying cake.*)

FLO. Helen, have you gone to the trouble of baking another cake?

MRS. POTTS. An old lady like me, if she wants any attention from the young men on a picnic, all she can do is bake a cake! I feel sort of excited, Flo. I think we plan picnics just to give ourselves an excuse . . . to let something thrilling and romantic happen to us ——

FLO. Such as what?

MRS. POTTS. I don't know. That's what's so exciting.

MADGE. (*Bursting out the front door, furious.*) Mom! Millie makes me furious! Every time she takes a bath, she fills up the whole bathtub. Now there isn't any hot water at all.

FLO. You should have thought of it earlier.

ROSEMARY. (*Hears Howard's car drive up and stop off* R. *She moves excitedly to* R. *edge of steps.*) It's him! It's him!

MRS. POTTS. (*Crosses* U. *to* U. L. *lawn, looks off* R.) Who? Oh, it's Howard. Hello, Howard!

ROSEMARY. (*Sitting down again in armchair.*) If he's been drinking, I'm not going out with him. (*Howard Bevans enters from alley* R. *He wears a panama hat, carries a lighted cigar and is in his shirtsleeves. Madge crosses* L. *to shed.*)

HOWARD. (*As he comes through alley gate.*) Howdy, ladies. Mrs. Owens ——

FLO. Hello, Howard. (*Mrs. Potts crosses* D., *sits on stump.*)

HOWARD. (*Crosses* D. *to* L. *of Rosemary.*) You sure look nice, Rosemary.

ROSEMARY. (*Her tone of voice must tell a man she is independent of him.*) Seems to me you might have left your coat on.

HOWARD. Still too darn hot, even if it is September. (*Turns to* L. *a step.*) Good evening, Madge.

38

MADGE. Hi, Howard.

FLO. How are things over in Cherryvale, Howard?

HOWARD. Good business. Back to school and everybody buying.

FLO. When business is good, it's good for everyone.

MILLIE. (*Comes out of kitchen, crosses shyly to* R. *of Howard.*) Hi, Howard!

HOWARD. (*To Flo, making a discovery.*) Hey, Millie's a good lookin' kid. I never realized it before. (*Flo sits in* C. *chair in yard.*)

MILLIE. (*Leaning over Flo, apprehensive.*) Mom, what time did the fellows say they'd be here?

FLO. At five-thirty. You've asked me a dozen times. (*A sound of approaching automobiles.*)

FLO. (*Looking off* R.) It's Alan! He's brought *both* cars! (*Millie runs into the house through front door. Rosemary crosses to* R. *edge of steps.*)

MRS. POTTS. One of these days you'll be riding around in that big Cadillac. (*Alan enters from* D. R.—*crosses to Flo.*)

ALAN. Everyone ready? (*Howard crosses* U. *on porch,* U. *of armchair.*)

FLO. Come sit down, Alan.

ROSEMARY. The more the merrier!

ALAN. I brought both cars. Hal's parking the Ford. (*The other car is heard stopping with a squeal of brakes.*) The trunk in the Cadillac won't hold everything. Whatever's left over, Hal and Millie can drive out in the Ford. (*To Madge, who is now sitting up on Mrs. Potts' porch railing.*) Hi, Beautiful!

MADGE. Hi, Alan!

ALAN. (*Calling off* R.) Hal!

FLO. Is he a careful driver, Alan? (*This question does not get answered. Hal comes running on* D. R., *tugging uncomfortably at the shoulders of his jacket. He crosses to Alan's* R.)

HAL. Hey, Seymour! (*Now he notices the crowd, realizes he was too noisy, and is more quiet.*) Look, Seymour, I'm a big man. I'm a lot huskier than you are. I can't wear your jacket.

ALAN. Then take it off. (*Hal does.*)

MRS. POTTS. Yes. I like to see a man comfortable.

HAL. (*With a broad smile of total confidence.*) I never could wear another fellow's clothes. See, I'm kinda beefy through the shoulders. (*He demonstrates the fact.*) I should have all my clothes

39

tailor made. (*He gives the coat to Alan and then swings his arms in appreciation of their new freedom. Mrs. Potts is admiring, the other women speculative.*)

ALAN. (*Clapping him on shoulder.*) Hey . . . uh . . . Hercules, you've met Mrs. Owens ——

HAL. (*Crosses below Alan to Flo.*) Oh, she's the mother!

ALAN. —And I believe you met Mrs. Potts this morning.

HAL. (*Crosses above to Mrs. Potts' L.—squats down—arms around her shoulders.*) Oh, she's my best girl!

MRS. POTTS. I baked a Lady Baltimore cake!

HAL. (*Expansively, as though making an announcement of public interest.*) This little lady, she took pity on me when I was practically starving. (*Rises, moves L. a step.*) I ran into some hard luck on my way here. Some characters robbed me of every cent I had. You see, these two characters ——

ALAN. (*Interrupting. Crosses to Rosemary—brings her to C.*) And . . . er . . . this is Rosemary Sydney, Hal. (*Hal crosses to Rosemary, Alan is above them.*) Miss Sydney teaches shorthand and typing in the local high school.

ROSEMARY. (*Offering her hand.*) Yes, I'm an old-maid schoolteacher.

HAL. (*With unnecessary earnestness.*) I have every respect for schoolteachers, Mam. It's a lotta hard work and not much pay. (*Rosemary cannot decide whether or not this is a compliment.*)

ALAN. (*Crosses U. to Howard.*) And this is Howard Bevans, Hal. (*Hal crosses U.—to L. of Howard.*) Mr. Bevans is a friend of Miss Sydney.

HOWARD. (*As they shake hands.*) I run a little shop over in Cherryvale. Notions, novelties and school supplies. You and Alan drive over sometime and get acquainted. (*Millie enters from front door and stands on the porch, elaborately pretending to be nonchalant and at ease.*)

HAL. (*To Howard, earnestly.*) Sir, we'll come over as soon as we can fit it into our schedule. (*He spies Millie.*) Hey, kid! (*Crosses D. to below steps, does an elaborate imitation of a swan dive and lands beside her on the porch.*) You got a little more tan today, didn't you? (*He hugs her affectionately. Howard steps D. onto lawn. Hal turns to the others, arm around Millie.*) You folks shoulda seen Millie this morning. She did a fine jackknife off the high diving board! (*General ad lib. congratulating Millie.*)

40

MILLIE. (*Breaking away, sitting on* R. *end of top step.*) Cut it out!
HAL. What'sa matter, kid? Think I'm snowin' you under? (*Gives her a playful push, rises to above steps on porch. To the whole group.*) I wouldn't admit this to many people, but she does a jack-knife almost as good as me! (*Realizes that this sounds bragging so goes on to explain.*) Oh, you see, I was diving champion on the West Coast, so I know what I'm talking about! (*This remark is a failure, too, and Hal admits as much by holding his nose and taking a flying leap onto the steps, sitting beside Millie. Rosemary sits on porch* L. *of armchair. Howard next to her at corner of porch.*)
FLO. (*After a moment.*) Madge, you should be getting dressed.
ALAN. Go on upstairs and get beautiful for us.
MADGE. Mom, can I wear my new dress?
FLO. No. I made you that dress to save for dances this fall. Go on, Madge.
MADGE. I will in a minute.
ROSEMARY. (*To Hal.*) Where'd you get those boots?
HAL. I guess maybe I ought to apologize for the way I look. But you see, those characters I told you about made off with all my clothes too. And I went to the police —— (*Alan steps toward Hal, who realizes he is on the wrong subject and stops.*)
MRS. POTTS. What a pity!
HAL. You see, the reason I brought the subject up was I just didn't want you folks to think you were associatin' with a bum. (*He covers his face, embarrassed.*) Oh, what the hell's the use!
MRS. POTTS. Clothes don't make the man.
FLO. Helen, is your mother taken care of?
MRS. POTTS. Yes, Flo. I've got a baby sitter for her.
FLO. Come on, Helen, let's start packing the baskets. (*She goes through kitchen door. Mrs. Potts rises to* D. L. *of stump but Hal's story fascinates her and she stops and turns.*)
HAL. (*To Mrs. Potts.*) See, Mam, my old man left me these boots when he died.
ROSEMARY. (*Impishly.*) That all he left you—just a pair of boots?
HAL. He gave me these boots and he said, "Son, the man of the house needs a pair of boots 'cause he's gotta do a lot of kickin'." (*He feints a kick at Millie. She flinches. He laughs goodnaturedly.*) And he made up a little poem.

41

"Your wages all are spent.
The landlord wants his rent.
You go to your woman for solace,
And she fills you fulla torment."

(*Mrs. Potts laughs—sits on stump.*) He says, "Son, there'll be times when the only thing you got to be proud of is the fact you're a man. (*Rises—crosses to* C.) So wear your boots and people can hear you comin', and keep your fists doubled up so they'll know you mean business when you get there." (*Clenches his fists, then relaxes with a laugh—looks round.*) My old man, he was a corker! (*He crosses* U. *on lawn* D. C.)

ALAN. (*Laughing.*) Hal's always so shy of people before he meets them. (*Sits in armchair.*) Then you can't keep still!

HAL. (*Laughing, agreeing with Alan.*) Yeah! (*He turns, sees Madge up on Mrs. Potts' porch railing.*) Hi!

MADGE. Hi!

HOWARD. What line of business you in, son?

HAL. (*Crosses* D., *turns* C. *chair in yard to face* D. R.) Sir, I'm about to enter the oil business. (*He sits on the chair,* C. *stage.*)

HOWARD. Oh!

HAL. (*Leans back.*) You see, while my old man was no aristocratic millionaire or anything, he had some very important friends who were very big men . . . in their own way. One of them wanted me to take a position with this oil company down in Texas, but ——

ALAN. (*Interrupting.*) Dad and I have found a place for Hal on the pipeline.

HAL. Gee, Seymour, I think you oughta let *me* tell the story.

ALAN. After all, Hal, these people aren't interested in your life history.

HAL. Yeah. (*Deflated, lets chair down, slumps low. Then begins quietly.*) So I've decided to start in from the very bottom. (*A pause.*) There's lots more important things in this life than money. I guess I've learned that much. (*A pause.*) But I certainly do appreciate this opportunity, (*Rises.*) and it's all due to Seymour and his old . . . father. (*Sits abruptly, embarrassed at his near mistake.*)

MRS. POTTS. (*Completely enraptured.*) I think that's wonderful!

HOWARD. It's a good business town. A young man can go far.

HAL. (*Regaining confidence.*) Sir, I intend to go far.

42

ROSEMARY. A young fellow just coming to town, he's gotta be a good mixer.

MRS. POTTS. Wouldn't it be nice if he could join the Country Club and play golf? (*Hal likes this idea, he sits forward.*)

ALAN. Oh, he won't be able to afford that. (*Hal nods in agreement, sits back, deflated.*)

ROSEMARY. The bowling team's a rowdy game! (*This sounds good to Hal.*)

MRS. POTTS. And there's a young men's Bible class at the Baptist Church. (*Hal gives a little frown. Flo enters from the kitchen, crosses to R. lawn.*)

FLO. Madge! Are you still here?

MADGE. (*Running across to the front door.*) If everyone will pardon me, I'll get dressed. (*She goes inside.*)

FLO. (*Crosses to D. C. lawn.*) It's about time.

ALAN. (*Calling after Madge.*) Hurry it up, will you, Delilah?

MILLIE. You oughta see the way Madge primps. She uses about six kinds of face cream and dusts herself all over with powder, and rubs perfume underneath her ears to make her real mysterious. It takes her half an hour —— (*She stops, confused.*) She won't be ready for hours.

FLO. Come on, Helen. (*Crosses to D. R. lawn.*) Alan, we're going to need a man to chip the ice and put the baskets in the car. (*Mrs. Potts crosses to kitchen door and exits.*)

HAL. (*Rising.*) I'll help you, Mam.

FLO. No, thank you. Alan—if you don't mind? (*Hal sits. Alan crosses to U. R. of Hal. Flo crosses to kitchen door.*)

ALAN. Mind your manners, Hal. (*He crosses U., holds kitchen door open for Flo.*)

MILLIE. (*Running up to corner of house.*) Mom!

FLO. (*Comes back to Millie.*) Why don't you show the young man your drawings?

MILLIE. (*Crosses to beach chair, turns to Hal.*) Wanta see my art?

HAL. You mean to tell me you can draw pictures? (*Millie gets her sketch pad from under beach chair. Flo exits to kitchen. Alan follows her. Kitchen porch light, kitchen light, front porch light, parlor light, all go on.*)

MILLIE. (*Crosses to Hal, opens pad to a sketch, hands pad to Hal.*) That's Mrs. Potts.

43

HAL. (*Impressed.*) Looks just like her.

MILLIE. I just love Mrs. Potts. When I go to heaven, I expect everyone to be just like her.

HAL. Hey, kid, wanta draw me?

MILLIE. (*Takes pad.*) Well, I'll try.

HAL. I had a job as a model once. (*Getting up on the stump.*) They made me pose raw in front of a whole class. (*Strikes a pose.*) How's this? (*Millie shakes her head.*) That's okay. I got plenty more. (*Sits on stump in another pose.*) Okay?

MILLIE. Why don't you just try to look natural?

HAL. Gee, that's hard. (*He thinks a moment, then bends way over to ground, shakes himself, slowly straightens up, resting his elbows easily on his thighs, head erect. Millie begins to sketch. Rosemary, becoming conscious of the brilliant sunlight from* R., *turns to look into it.*)

ROSEMARY. Howard, look at that sunset!

HOWARD. (*Turns to look.*) Pretty, isn't it?

ROSEMARY. That's the most flaming sunset I ever did see.

HOWARD. If you painted that in a picture, no one'd believe you.

ROSEMARY. It's like the daylight didn't want to end, isn't it?

HOWARD. (*Not fully aware of what she means.*) Oh . . . I don't know.

ROSEMARY. Like the daytime was gonna put up a big scrap and maybe set the world on fire . . . to keep night-time from creepin' on.

HOWARD. Uh-huh . . . I think I see what you mean there. Uh-huh . . .

HAL. (*As Millie sketches him he starts thinking out loud.*) You know, there comes a time in a guy's life when he's gotta settle down . . . quit rolling around like a pinball.

ROSEMARY. No, Howard, if Millie's going to be here, I don't think there ought to be any drinking.

HAL. (*Turns.*) What's that?

ROSEMARY. Nothing.

HAL. (*To Millie.*) Hey, kid, what'd you do this afternoon?

MILLIE. Read a book.

HAL. You read a whole book in one afternoon?

MILLIE. Sure. Hold still.

HAL. I'm a son of a gun. What was it about?

MILLIE. Well, it's kind of hard to explain, it's just the way you feel when you read it—kind of warm inside and sad and amused—all at the same time.

HAL. Yeah . . . sure. (*After a moment proudly.*) I used to go with a girl once who read books. She joined the Book-of-the-Month Club and they had her readin' books all the time! She wouldn't any more than finish one book than they'd send her another! (*Howard rises and crosses* u. *to alley gate.*)

ROSEMARY. Where you goin', Howard?

HOWARD. I'll be right back, Honey. (*He exits* R. *alley. Rosemary follows him to* u. *porch chair and kneels on chair, and watches him while he is off.*)

HAL. (*As Millie hands him the sketch.*) Not bad. (*Admiring it.*) I sure do admire people who are artistic. Can I keep it?

MILLIE. Sure. (*Rises, takes pad, stops, shyly.*) I write poetry, too. I've written poems I've never shown to a living soul.

HAL. No kidding.

ROSEMARY. (*Calling off to Howard.*) Howard, leave that bottle right where it is! (*Millie tears sketch out of pad.*)

HAL. (*Jumps up, crosses* u. *to* u. c. *lawn.*) Did she say "bottle"?

ROSEMARY. (*Coming down to Hal.*) He's been down to the hotel, buying bootleg whiskey off those good-for-nothing porters! (*She crosses to* R. *lawn.*)

HOWARD. (*Coming back from alley* R., *holding out a bottle, to Hal's* R.) Young man, maybe you'd like a swig of this.

HAL. Hot damn! (*He takes the bottle, takes a swig.*)

ROSEMARY. Howard, put that away. (*Hal crosses* D., *puts* L. *foot on stump, takes a drink. Howard crosses* D. *to* D. c. *lawn.*)

HOWARD. Millie's not gonna be shocked if she sees someone take a drink. Are you, Millie?

MILLIE. Gosh, no! (*She gives the sketch to Hal. Hal looks at it, folds it, puts it in his pocket.*)

ROSEMARY. (*Crosses to below steps.*) What if someone'd come by and tell the school board? I'd lose my job quick as you can say Jack Robinson.

HOWARD. Who's gonna see you, Honey? Everyone in town's at the picnic.

ROSEMARY. (*Crosses to* c.) I don't care. Liquor's against the law in this state, and a person oughta abide by the law. (*To Hal.*) Isn't that what you say, young fellow?

45

HAL. Oh, sure! A person oughta abide by the law. (*He hands the bottle to Howard.*)

HOWARD. Here, Honey.

ROSEMARY. (*Crosses to below steps.*) No, Howard, I'm not gonna touch a drop.

HOWARD. One little drink won't hurt you.

ROSEMARY. I said "no" and I mean "no."

HOWARD. Come on, Honey, have one little drink just for *me*. (*Bumps her with his knee.*)

ROSEMARY. (*Beginning to melt.*) Howard, you oughta be ashamed of yourself.

HOWARD. (*Innocent.*) I don't see why.

ROSEMARY. I guess I know why you want me to take a drink.

HOWARD. Now, Honey, that's not so. I just think you should have a good time like the rest of us. (*To Hal, crosses L. to C.*) Schoolteachers gotta right to live. Right?

HAL. Right! (*Howard turns back to Rosemary.*)

ROSEMARY. Now, Millie, don't you tell any of the kids at school.

MILLIE. (*Disgusted at being taken for a child.*) What do you take me for? (*Hal puts arm around Millie.*)

ROSEMARY. Anyone coming? (*Crosses U. to R. of front door.*)

HOWARD. (*Looks around.*) Coast is clear. (*Crosses U. to Rosemary, gives her the bottle.*)

ROSEMARY. (*Takes a hearty drink.*) Whew! I want some water!

HOWARD. (*Crosses to C.*) Millie, why don't you run in the house and get her some? (*Millie starts up.*)

ROSEMARY. No, Howard! I'll get a drink from the hydrant! (*She runs off to Mrs. Potts' yard D. L. Millie comes D. to above and between Hal and Howard.*)

HOWARD. Millie, my girl, I'd like to offer you one, but I'm afraid your old lady'd raise Ned.

MILLIE. What Mom don't know won't hurt her! (*She reaches for the bottle.*)

HAL. (*He grabs the bottle first.*) No, kid. You lay off the stuff! (*Crosses U. to L. of tree. He takes a drink.*)

ROSEMARY. (*Calling from offstage L.*) Howard, come help me! I see a snake!

HOWARD. You go, Millie. She don't see no snake. (*Millie goes off D. L.*) Drink up. (*As Hal takes another drink, he sees a light go on in Madge's window. Howard follows Hal's gaze.*) Look at her there, powdering her arms. I was in love with a pretty girl like her once. You know, every time I come over here I look forward just to seein' her. I tell myself, "Bevans, old boy, you can look at that all you want, but you couldn't touch it with a ten-foot pole."

HAL. I'm glad Seymour's got such a nice babe—'cause he's my buddy.

HOWARD. Seymour's a young pup. He'll go off to school soon and forget all about her.

HAL. Gee, I don't see how anyone could forget *her*.

HOWARD. Look at her, putting lipstick on that cute kisser. They tell me every boy in town has been on the make for that since she was old enough to go to Sunday School. Seems to me, when the good Lord made a girl as pretty as she is, He did it for a reason, and it's about time she found out what that reason is. (*He gets an idea.*) Look, son, if you're agonizin', I know a couple of girls down at the hotel.

HAL. Thanks a lot but you see, I never had to pay for it.

HOWARD. I think that's a very fine attitude. (*Rosemary enters D. L. followed by Millie.*)

ROSEMARY. (*Crosses to C.*) Lord, I thought I was going to faint!

MILLIE. (*Leans against trellis L.*) It was just a piece of garden hose.

ROSEMARY. (*Suspiciously.*) What've you two been talking about?

HOWARD. Talkin' about the weather, Honey.

ROSEMARY. I bet.

MILLIE. (*Seeing Madge in the window, crosses to R. C. lawn.*) Hey, Madge, why don't you charge admission? (*Madge's curtains close.*)

ROSEMARY. (*Sits C. chair.*) Shoot! When I was a girl I was just as good looking as she is! (*Music begins to play off L.*)

HOWARD. Of course you were, Honey.

ROSEMARY. (*Taking the bottle.*) If my father had ever caught me showing off in front of a window he'd have tanned me with a razor strap. (*She takes a drink.*)

HOWARD. 'Course, Honey.

ROSEMARY. 'Cause he was a God-fearing man.

MILLIE. Listen, Miss Sidney, it's Ernie Higgins and his Happiness

47

Boys. (*She crosses up to* U. C. *lawn.*) Hey, hit it, Ernie! (*She crosses* D. *to* L. *of porch corner.*)

ROSEMARY. (*Rises, handing bottle to Howard, begins to sway rapturously.*) Lord, I love that music! Come dance with me, Howard!

HOWARD. Honey, I'm no good at dancin'.

ROSEMARY. That's just what you menfolks tell yourselves to get out of it. (*Turns to Millie.*) Come dance with me, Millie! (*She pulls Millie up onto the porch and they push the chairs out of the way. Howard sits on stump and starts drinking. Hal begins to dance by himself, sensuously—facing the shed.*)

MILLIE. I gotta lead! (*Rosemary and Millie dance together in a trim, automatic way that keeps time to the music but little else. Both women seem to show a little arrogance in dancing together, as though boasting to the men of their independence. Their rhythm is accurate but uninspired. Howard looks up at them.*)

HOWARD. S'posin' Hal and I did that.

ROSEMARY. Go ahead for all I care. (*Howard rises, puts the bottle by the tree, taps Hal on the shoulder. Hal turns and Howard holds out his arms ceremoniously. Hal turns, twists away in exaggerated shyness then takes Howard's hands and they start dancing together, Hal giving his own clown's version of a coy female. Rosemary is irritated by this. She and Millie stop dancing and watch. Hal and Howard circle over to* C. *Rosemary crosses* L. *to them and grabs Howard's shoulder.*) Stop it!

HOWARD. I thought we were doin' very nicely. (*Rosemary grabs Howard and pulls him up on the porch where they dance. Hal picks up* C. *chair and puts it up out of the way.*)

HAL. Hey, Millie! Come and dance with me!

MILLIE. Well . . . I never danced with boys.

HAL. Honest?

MILLIE. I always have to lead.

HAL. Just relax and do the steps I do. Come on and try. (*They dance together but Millie has an awkward feeling of uncertainty that shows in her dancing. Howard, dancing with Rosemary, has been cutting up.*)

ROSEMARY. (*Stops, pushes him off.*) Quit clowning, Howard, and dance with me.

HOWARD. Honey, you don't get any fun out of dancing with me. (*Rosemary and Howard begin to dance again.*)

48

MILLIE. (*Stops and says to Hal:*) Am I too bad?

HAL. Naw! You just need a little practice. (*They begin again, dancing L. to below stump.*)

ROSEMARY. (*She is dancing with Howard but her words are meant for Hal.*) Lord, I love to dance. At school, kids all called me the Dancin' Fool. Went somewhere dancin' every night! (*Mrs. Potts enters from kitchen, crosses to C. chair.*)

MRS. POTTS. (*Watching.*) I can't stay in the kitchen while there's dancing! (*She turns C. chair and sits watching. Alan enters from kitchen wearing an apron. He watches Millie then signals to Flo off stage.*)

HAL. (*Stops L. of stump to deliver the needed instructions, foot on stump.*) Now look, kid, you gotta remember I'm the man, and the man always leads in everything. (*Millie nods. Hal takes her again and they begin to circle faster and faster, C. stage. As they dance, Flo enters from kitchen and stands on back porch next to Alan. They both watch approvingly.*)

MRS. POTTS. You're doing fine, Millie!

MILLIE. (*Her head back as she is whirled around.*) I feel like Rita Hayworth! (*Flo and Alan go into the kitchen. Millie and Hal stop turning and do jitterbug.*)

HAL. You're doin' great, kid!

ROSEMARY. One night I went dancin' at a big Valentine party. I danced so hard I swooned! That's when they called me the Dancin' Fool.

HAL. (*Stops dancing for a moment.*) I'll show you a new step, Kid. I learned this in L. A. Try it. (*He nimbly executes a somewhat more intricate step.*)

MRS. POTTS. Isn't he graceful?

MILLIE. Gee, that looks hard.

HAL. Takes a little time. Give it a try! (*Millie tries to do it, but it is too much for her.*)

MILLIE. (*Giving up. She crosses D. R. below steps.*) I'm sorry, but that one's just too hard.

HAL. The hell with it! (*He runs to tree, picks up the whiskey bottle and takes a drink, putting the bottle back on Mrs. Potts' steps. He crosses D., beckoning to Millie.*) Look, kid, if you learn this step you'll be the sharpest kid in town. (*He places her far L. and does a step back and forth below stump.*)

MILLIE. (*Observing closely.*) Yah . . . but . . .

49

HAL. Real loose, see? You give it a little of this . . . and give it a little of this. (*Now the music changes to a slower, more sensuous rhythm. Hal and Millie stop dancing and listen to it.*)

ROSEMARY. Howard, this is the way to dance!

HOWARD. Sure! (*Hal starts to do the same step to the slow rhythm and Millie tries to imitate him.*)

MILLIE. Gee, I hope I can get it! (*Madge enters from front door, wearing her new dress. She looks ravishing. She watches Hal and Millie.*)

HOWARD. You sure look pretty, Madge.

MADGE. Thank you, Howard.

HOWARD. Madge, would you like a little dance? (*Madge accepts, and they dance together on the porch. Rosemary is dancing by herself on the porch, upstage, and does not notice them. Millie continues to attempt step Hal is doing.*)

MRS. POTTS. (*Sees Madge and Howard dancing.*) More dancers! We've turned the backyard into a ballroom!

ROSEMARY. (*Dances down to Howard and claims him from Madge.*) Thought you couldn't dance. (*Madge goes down into the yard and watches Hal and Millie.*)

MRS. POTTS. (*To Madge.*) The young man is teaching Millie a new step.

MADGE. I've been trying to teach it to Alan. (*She tries the step herself and does it as well as Hal. She is far* D. S.)

MRS. POTTS. Look, everyone! Madge can do it, too!

HAL. (*Turns around and sees Madge dancing.*) Hey! (*He starts to dance toward her. She begins also. The others all stand riveted as they watch Madge and Hal dance to each other, go through a slow graceful jitterbug routine at* C. *and then dance to far* L. *where they continue to dance a conventional step, close together, forgetting the others completely.*)

MRS. POTTS. It's like they were made to dance together, isn't it? (*This remark breaks the spell. Millie moves to Mrs. Potts' steps and sits quietly in the background.*)

ROSEMARY. Can't you dance that way?

HOWARD. Me? No.

ROSEMARY. Then keep out of my way! (*Rosemary dances by herself, kicking her legs in the air. Millie takes an occasional drink from the whiskey bottle during the following scene, unobserved by the others.*) I danced so hard one night, I swooned! Right in the center of the ballroom!

HOWARD. Rosemary's got pretty legs, hasn't she?

ROSEMARY. Can't you men talk about anything but women's legs?

HOWARD. I just noticed they had a good shape.

ROSEMARY. How would you like it if we women went around talkin' 'bout *your* legs all the time?

HOWARD. (*Ready to be a sport, stands and lifts his trousers to his knees.*) All right! There's my legs if you wanta talk about them.

ROSEMARY. (*She explodes with laughter.*) Never saw anything so ugly. Men's big hairy legs! (*Crosses D. off steps.*) Never saw anything so ugly! (*Rosemary goes over to Hal, who is still dancing with Madge.*) Young man, let's see your legs. (*She pushes them apart. They are both startled.*)

HAL. (*Concerned with Madge, is startled.*) Huh?

ROSEMARY. We passed a new rule here tonight. Every man here's gotta show his legs. (*She pulls Hal's R. trouser leg out of the boot.*)

HOWARD. (*Crosses D. to below steps.*) Honey, he's got on boots.

ROSEMARY. Okay, then he's gotta dance with me. I may be an old maid schoolteacher, but I can keep up with you. Come on, cowboy! (*Madge retreats to the side as Rosemary pulls Hal to her. He dances with her.*) I used to have a boy friend was a cowboy. Met him out in Colorado. He was in love with me 'cause I was an older woman and had some sense. (*They turn.*) Took me up in the mountains once and proposed. Wanted me to marry him right there on the mountain top. Said God'd be our preacher, the moon our best man. Ever hear such talk? Didja? Didja? (*Hal pulls away from her.*) Where you goin'? You gotta dance with me! (*Rosemary holds on desperately.*)

HAL. Mam, I guess I just don't feel like dancing.

ROSEMARY. I can keep up with you! I can keep up with you!

HOWARD. Rosemary! Rosemary! (*He tries to pull her away from Hal as Rosemary holds onto Hal's shirt collar. As Howard breaks her loose from Hal she rips the whole side out of Hal's shirt.*) He's dancing with Madge. They're *young* people. (*Madge crosses to Hal—helps him tuck in torn shirt tail.*)

51

ROSEMARY. (*Stunned by Hal's rejection.*) Young? What do you mean, they're young?

MILLIE. (*A groan.*) Oh, I'm sick!

MRS. POTTS. (*Rising.*) Millie!

MILLIE. (*Crossing towards the kitchen.*) I wanna die! I wanna die! (*Hal quickly moves* c. *chair up against side of Potts' steps and stands* L. *of Madge and Millie.*)

MADGE. Millie!

HOWARD. What'd the little Dickens do? Get herself tight?

HAL. Take it easy, kid.

ROSEMARY. I suppose that's something wonderful—they're young.

MADGE. (*Arm around Millie.*) Let's go inside, Millie.

MILLIE. (*Turning on Madge and pushing her off. Hal catches Madge before she falls.*) I hate you!

MADGE. (*Hurt.*) Millie!

MILLIE. (*Sobbing, she crosses to kitchen door.*) Madge is the pretty one . . . Madge is the pretty one. (*She goes inside.*)

MRS. POTTS. Millie! (*She follows her in. Howard crosses to bottle on Mrs. Potts' steps.*)

MADGE. (*Crosses* D. R. *to below steps.*) Mom is going to be furious.

HOWARD. (*Examining the bottle, turns to others.*) She must have had several good snifters. (*Hal crosses slowly to Madge.*)

ROSEMARY. (*Pointing a finger at Hal. She has found vengeance. She crosses to* D. C. *lawn.*) It's all his fault, Howard.

HOWARD. Now, Honey . . .

ROSEMARY. (*To Hal, defiantly and accusingly.*) Millie was your date. You shoulda been looking after her. But you were too busy making eyes at Madge.

HOWARD. Honey . . .

ROSEMARY. . . . and you're no better than he is, Madge. You should be ashamed.

MADGE. Miss Sidney!

FLO. (*Flies out on the kitchen porch in a fury.*) Who fed whiskey to my Millie?

ROSEMARY. He did, Mrs. Owens! It's all his fault! (*Flo glares at Hal.*)

MADGE. (*Crosses* U. *on steps.*) Mother, that's not so!

HOWARD. (*Trying to straighten things out.*) Mrs. Owens, it was this way ——

FLO. My Millie is too young to be drinking whiskey!

ROSEMARY. Oh, he'd have fed her whiskey and taken his pleasure with the child and then skidaddled!

HOWARD. Now listen, everyone. Let's ——

ROSEMARY. I know what I'm doing, Howard! (*Back at Hal.*) You been stomping around here in those boots like you owned the place, thinking every woman you saw was gonna fall madly in love. But here's one woman who didn't pay you any mind. (*She stumbles* D. *off the lawn* D. C.)

HOWARD. The boy hasn't done anything, Mrs. Owens!

ROSEMARY. Aristocratic millionaire, my foot! You wouldn't know an aristocratic millionaire if he spit on you. You're just a piece of Arkansas white trash! And braggin' about your father! And I'll bet he wasn't any better'n you are! I'll bet you lose that job before your two weeks is up.

HOWARD. None of us saw Millie drink the whiskey!

ROSEMARY. You think just 'cause you're young you can push the old folks aside. You'll end your life in a gutter and it'll serve you right, 'cause the gutter's where you came from and the gutter's where you belong —— (*During this she crosses to Hal and shouts the last right in his face. Howard crosses to her quickly.*)

HOWARD. (*Grabs Rosemary, covering her mouth.*) Rosemary, shut your mouth! (*He pulls her away to far* L.)

MRS. POTTS. (*Comes out of kitchen.*) Millie's going to be perfectly all right, Flo. Alan held her head and let her be sick. She's going to be perfectly all right now. (*Alan and Millie enter from kitchen. He has his arm around her.*)

FLO. (*A general announcement.*) I want it understood that there's to be no more drinking on this picnic.

HOWARD. It was all my fault, Mrs. Owens. My fault.

MRS. POTTS. Here's Millie now, good as new. And we're all going on the picnic and forget it. (*Flo crosses to Millie.*)

ALAN. (*Quick to accuse Hal.*) Hal, what happened?

FLO. (*To Alan.*) Alan, Millie will come with us.

ALAN. Sure, Mrs. Owens. Hal, I told you not to drink!

FLO. Madge, why did you wear your new dress?

MADGE. I don't know. I just put it on.

53

FLO. Go upstairs and change, this minute. I mean it! You come with Rosemary and Howard! (*Madge runs inside front door.*)

MRS. POTTS. Let's go. All the tables will be taken.

FLO. Alan, help me with Millie. Millie, darling, are you feeling better? (*Flo and Millie go off alley R.*)

MRS. POTTS. Young man, you follow their car ——

ALAN. Oh, Mr. Bevans, will you tell Madge I'll see her out there. (*He exits alley R.*)

MRS. POTTS. —I mean our car. Oh, dear. (*Mrs. Potts follows the others off alley R. We hear the Cadillac drive off. Hal is sitting silent and beaten on the edge of the porch. Howard and Rosemary are by the shed.*)

HOWARD. He's just a boy, Rosemary. You talked awful.

ROSEMARY. (*Crosses below stump then u. to u. c. lawn.*) Howard, what made me do it? What made me act that way?

HOWARD. You gotta remember, men have got feelings, too— same as women. (*To Hal, crosses to above stump.*) Don't pay any attention to her, young man. She didn't mean a thing.

ROSEMARY. I don't want to go on the picnic, Howard. This is my last night of vacation and I want to have a good time.

HOWARD. (*Crosses u. for the bottle.*) Anything you say, dear.

ROSEMARY. I wanta go for a ride, Howard. I want to drive into the sunset! I want to drive into the sunset! (*She runs off towards the car, through alley R., Howard following. Howard's car drives away. Hal starts to rise. Madge comes out front door. She is wearing another dress. Hal quickly sits again. She sits on the bench on the porch and finally speaks in a gentle voice.*)

MADGE. Don't feel bad. Women like Miss Sydney make me disgusted with the whole female sex. (*Recalling something, smiling.*) Last year she and some of the other teachers made such a fuss about a statue in the library. It was a gladiator and all he had on was a shield on his arm. Those teachers kept hollering about that statue, they said it was an insult to them every time they walked into the library. Finally, they made the principal—I don't know how to say it, but one of the janitors got busy with a chisel and then they weren't insulted any more. The next day there was a sign hanging on the statue—"Miss Sydney was here." I know you're not in the mood for funny stories, but you just have to laugh at Miss Sydney.

HAL. What's the use, Baby? She saw through me like an X-ray

machine. I'm a *bum!* There's just no place in the world for a guy like me.

MADGE. I know how you feel. Millie's so smart and talented. I get to feeling so jealous of her and worthless when I try to be like her. Then I tell myself that I'm not Millie—I'm *me!* And I feel lots better.

HAL. I'm *me*.

MADGE. Sure!

HAL. Sure. But what's that?

MADGE. (*Rises—crosses to* U. L. *of Hal.*) Well, you're very entertaining. I mean . . . I think you say all sorts of witty things. And you're a wonderful dancer.

HAL. What good's dancin'?

MADGE. Oh, I can tell a lot about a boy by dancing with him.

HAL. You can?

MADGE. Some boys, even though they're very smart, when they take a girl in their arms to dance, they're kind of awkward and she feels sort of uncomfortable.

HAL. She does?

MADGE. (*She sits at his* L.) But when you took me in your arms to dance, I had the most wonderful feeling you knew exactly where you were going and I could follow every step of the way. So you're not so bad. I don't care what you say.

HAL. Oh, yeah? (*He turns to face her.*) Look, kid, lemme level with you. When I was fourteen I spent a year in a reform school. How do you like that?

MADGE. What for?

HAL. I stole a guy's motorcycle. Yeah, I stole it. I got no excuses. I stole it 'cause I wanted to get on the damn thing and go so far away, so fast, that nothin' would ever catch up with me.

MADGE. Sure.

HAL. Then my old lady went to the authorities. "I've done everything I can with the boy," she says. "I can't do another thing with him." So off I go to the damn reform school. And the old lady's real happy 'cause my Dad's always loaded and she's got a new boy friend and I'm in the way.

MADGE. (*She turns away.*) Gee . . .

HAL. Well, there you are. And I never told anybody about that—not even Seymour—'cause Seymour's Seymour and I'm . . . me. So if you want to get sick or run inside and lock your door or faint . . . go ahead. I ain't gonna stop you 'cause —— (*Madge suddenly kisses him. After the kiss he looks at her a moment.*) Gee, baby, you come out here on the porch lookin' like a pretty little doll, but you're a real woman, aren't you?

MADGE. I want to be.

HAL. You are.

MADGE. Am I? (*Now Hal kisses her. After a moment Madge breaks away and walks over near Mrs. Potts' steps. Hal follows to her R., turns her to him.*) We gotta go on the picnic.

HAL. Do we? There's other places . . . with not so many people. (*He pulls her to him and kisses her passionately. He releases her, then goes upstage and looks off R. and L. to see that no one is around. He turns to Madge and holds out his hand to her. After a moment she gives him her hand and they walk off slowly together through alley R.*)

CURTAIN

ACT III

SCENE 1

It is after midnight. A great harvest moon shines in the sky, a deep, murky blue. The moon is swollen and full and casts a pale light on the scene below. The light on Flo's porch is burning. A stick lies on the lawn at R. near the porch. Off R. we hear Howard's Chevrolet chugging to a stop by the house, then Howard and Rosemary come on R. through alley, Rosemary first. Wearily, a groggy depression having set in, she makes her way to the doorstep and drops there, sitting on porch corner. Howard enters quickly as she sits. He crosses D. to D. C. lawn. She seems preoccupied at first and her responses to Howard are mere grunts.

HOWARD. Here we are, Honey. Right back where we started from.

ROSEMARY. (*Her mind elsewhere.*) Uhh.

HOWARD. (*Sits at her L. on porch edge.*) You were awful nice to me tonight, Rosemary.

ROSEMARY. Uhh.

HOWARD. Do you think Mrs. Owens suspects anything?

ROSEMARY. I don't care if she does.

HOWARD. (*Rises, crosses L. to C.*) A business man's gotta be careful of talk. And after all, you're a schoolteacher. (*Fumbling to get away.*) Well, I guess I better be gettin' back to Cherryvale. I gotta open up the store in the morning. (*Crosses to her.*) Good night, Rosemary. Good night. (*He kisses her cheek.*) Maybe I should say, good morning. (*He starts off—crosses to U. C. lawn.*)

ROSEMARY. (*Just coming to.*) Where you goin', Howard?

HOWARD. (*Crosses D. a bit.*) Honey, I gotta get home.

ROSEMARY. You can't go off and leave me.

HOWARD. (*Crosses D. to D. C. lawn.*) Honey, talk sense.

57

ROSEMARY. You can't go off without me. Not after tonight. *That's* sense.

HOWARD. (*A little nervous.*) Honey, be reasonable.

ROSEMARY. Take me with you.

HOWARD. What'd people say?

ROSEMARY. (*Almost vicious.*) To *hell* with what people'd say!

HOWARD. (*Shocked—looks around to see if this is overheard.*) Honey!

ROSEMARY. What'd people say if I thumbed my nose at them? What'd people say if I walked down the street and showed 'em my pink panties? What do I care what people say?

HOWARD. (*Crosses D. to R. of stump.*) Honey, you're not yourself tonight.

ROSEMARY. Yes I am. I'm more myself than I ever was. Take me with you, Howard. If you don't, I don't know what I'll do with myself. I mean it.

HOWARD. (*Crosses to her, leans over her.*) Now look, Honey, you better go upstairs and get some sleep. You gotta start school in the morning. We'll talk all this over Saturday.

ROSEMARY. (*Grabs his arms.*) Maybe you won't be back Saturday. Maybe you won't be back ever again.

HOWARD. (*Pulling away a step.*) Rosemary, you know better than that.

ROSEMARY. (*Front.*) Then what's the next thing in store for me? To be nice to the next man, then the next . . . till there's no one left to care whether I'm nice to him or not. Till I'm ready for the grave and don't have anyone to take me there.

HOWARD. (*Crosses L. to C. ridge.*) Now, Rosemary!

ROSEMARY. (*Looking him in the eyes.*) You can't let that happen to me, Howard.

HOWARD. I don't understand. When we first started going together, you were the best sport I ever saw, always good for a laugh.

ROSEMARY. I can't laugh any more.

HOWARD. (*Starts u. s.*) We'll talk it over Saturday.

ROSEMARY. We'll talk it over *now*.

HOWARD. (*Stops, crosses D., sits on stump. Squirming.*) Well . . . Honey . . . I . . .

ROSEMARY. (*Looking at him.*) You said you were gonna marry me, Howard. You said when I got back from my vacation, you'd be waitin' with the preacher.

HOWARD. Honey, I've had an awful busy summer and . . .

ROSEMARY. Where's the preacher, Howard? Where is he?

HOWARD. Rosemary, I'm 42 years old. A person forms certain ways of livin', then one day it's too late to change.

ROSEMARY. (Rises, crosses to C.) I'm no spring chicken either. Maybe I'm a little older than you think I am. I've formed my ways, too. But they can be changed. (Turns, crosses R. to steps.) They gotta be changed. It's no good livin' like this, in rented rooms, meetin' a bunch of old maids for supper every night, then comin' back home alone.

HOWARD. (Rises, crosses to C.) I know how it is, Rosemary. My life's no bed of roses either.

ROSEMARY. (Turning to him.) Then why don't you do something about it?

HOWARD. I figure . . . there's some bad things about every life.

ROSEMARY. There's too much bad about mine. Each year, I keep tellin' myself, is the last. Something'll happen. Then nothing ever does . . . except I get a little crazier all the time.

HOWARD. (Hopelessly.) Well . . .

ROSEMARY. A well's a hole in the ground, Howard.

HOWARD. I wasn't tryin' to be funny, Rosemary.

ROSEMARY. All this time you just been leadin' me on.

HOWARD. (Vehement.) Rosemary, that's not so! I've not been trying to lead you on.

ROSEMARY. I'd like to know what else you call it.

HOWARD. Well . . . can't we talk about it Saturday? I'm dead tired and I got a busy week ahead, and . . .

ROSEMARY. (Runs to him, embraces him desperately.) You gotta marry me, Howard.

HOWARD. (Tortured.) Well . . . I can't marry you now.

ROSEMARY. (Looking at him.) You can be over here in the morning.

HOWARD. Sometimes you're unreasonable.

ROSEMARY. You gotta marry me.

HOWARD. What'll you do about your job?

ROSEMARY. (Encouraged.) Alvah Jackson can take my place till they get someone new from the agency.

HOWARD. I'll have to pay Fred Jenkins to take care of the store for a few days.

ROSEMARY. Then get him.

HOWARD. (*Turns away* D. L.) Well . . .

ROSEMARY. I'll be waitin' for you in the morning, Howard.

HOWARD. (*After a moment's troubled thought crosses to* D. L. *of steps.*) No. I'm not gonna marry anyone that says, "You gotta marry me, Howard." I'm not gonna. (*He is silent. Rosemary stares at him. Slowly Howard reconsiders.*) If a woman wants me to marry her . . . she could at least say "please."

ROSEMARY. (*Beaten and humble.*) Please marry me, Howard.

HOWARD. Well . . . you got to give me time to think it over.

ROSEMARY. Oh, God! Please marry me, Howard. Please. . . . (*She sinks to her knees.*) Please . . . please . . .

HOWARD. (*Turns.*) Rosemary, don't! (*He goes to her, lifts her up.*) Honey, you go get some sleep. I'll call you in the morning.

ROSEMARY. I won't sleep a wink, Howard, till I hear. (*He lifts her gently to her feet. She crosses to steps at* R.—U. *on top step.*) Good night, Howard.

HOWARD. I'll call you first thing. (*Crosses to her—squeezes her hand.*)

ROSEMARY. Good night.

HOWARD. 'Night, Rosemary. (*Crosses* U. C. *lawn.*)

ROSEMARY. (*Holding in her tears.*) Please call.

HOWARD. (*Turning back a step.*) I'll call. (*He starts again.*)

ROSEMARY. Please call.

HOWARD. (*Stops.*) I will, Rosemary. I will. (*Starts.*)

ROSEMARY. Please call.

HOWARD. (*Stops.*) Honey, don't worry.

ROSEMARY. Good night.

HOWARD. Good night. (*He is gone out alley* R. *As we hear Howard's car drive off. Rosemary silently looks up at the sky. Then she turns and goes silently into the house, turning off the porch light. The stage is empty and quiet for a few moments. Then we hear Alan's Ford drive up and stop off beyond Mrs. Potts' house. The car door slams. Then Hal enters through alley* L., *comes on quietly to* L. *of stump. He looks around, then turns and beckons.*)

HAL. Okay. (*Madge enters from alley* L., *touches him—he responds. She passes him to* D. R. *of stump.*) I'll take the car back to where we were and get a little sleep. I can't go back to Seymour's house now.

MADGE. No.

HAL. I didn't even think of Seymour 'til just this second.

MADGE. I don't think either of us thought much about anything. (*She looks toward him and then* R. *again.*)

HAL. (*Gently, with deepest intimacy.*) Are you all right, baby?

MADGE. (*Slowly.*) Yes . . . I'm all right.

HAL. Will I . . . see you tomorrow?

MADGE. I don't know.

HAL. I almost forgot. I start a new job this morning.

MADGE. I have to be at the dime store at nine.

HAL. What time you through?

MADGE. Six.

HAL. Will I see you?

MADGE. I don't know.

HAL. Well . . . I guess I better be going.

MADGE. I guess so.

HAL. (*He starts—turns back suddenly.*) Baby, how you goin' to handle your mother?

MADGE. I don't know.

HAL. Oh . . .

MADGE. (*Touching his shoulder.*) Don't worry.

HAL. (*He takes her hand. She pulls it away. He crosses* R. *below her to* C., *turns back to her,* L. *foot on stump, takes her hand. His head is down.*) Baby, you don't mind goin' with a guy who's workin' on the pipeline, do you?

MADGE. Don't be silly.

HAL. (*Looking up.*) I'm really happier with a job like that, one I can really handle, than I would be pretendin' to be a big-shot.

MADGE. It can have just as much future as any other kind of job.

HAL. (*As though he just realized it, taking both her hands.*) Sure. A guy gets spoiled if he's a good football player or something. He thinks he can expect his whole life to be big-time, but . . . (*Like a sigh of relief.*) Gee, I'm lucky I met you. I feel *fine.* Like comin' down through the clouds in your parachute, landin' solid on the ground, and the old world feels pretty good to my feet again. (*He laughs, then looks at her, takes her by waist.*) Baby, are you cryin'? (*Their foreheads together.*)

MADGE. Just a little. (*There are tears in her eyes.*)

HAL. Why?

MADGE. I don't know.

61

HAL. (*A lump in his throat.*) You almost got me doin' it.

MADGE. It's not 'cause I'm unhappy, really.

HAL. Same here. I'm not unhappy.

MADGE. (*Pulls away to* C.) It's just that ——

HAL. (*Crosses to her* L.—*hand on her arm.*) Baby, kiss me good night.

MADGE. It'd just start things all over again.

HAL. Well . . . kiss me good night anyway, will you?

MADGE. If you promise not to hold me?

HAL. Yah. I promise. I'll keep my hands at my side. See?

MADGE. Now I'll kiss you. (*Tenderly she takes his face in her hand and kisses him on the mouth. The kiss is extended. Then Hal's hands become nervous. They fidget at his sides and finally begin to find their way around her. He pulls away then begins to lose ground again—finally embraces her fiercely. For a moment their passion is revived. Then Madge tears herself away from him, and runs inside the front door. Hal stands looking after her, breathless. The stage darkens until we cannot see him.*)

CURTAIN

ACT III

SCENE 2

It is very early the next morning. Millie sits on the doorstep, smoking her after-breakfast cigarette. Flo comes out front door almost immediately. She is a near-hysterical woman now. She has not even taken the time to dress, and wears a long robe over her night dress.

FLO. (*Sits in armchair on porch.*) Madge has still got her door locked. I holler in but I can't get her to answer. I can't understand why I didn't hear her come in last night. I was sitting right there. I thought I was awake.

MILLIE. I bet I know what happened.

FLO. (*Vindictive.*) You don't know anything, Millie Owens! And if anyone should say anything to you, you just ——

MRS. POTTS. (*Comes out of her house on her porch.*) Is Madge all right?

FLO. (*Suspiciously.*) What do you mean?

MRS. POTTS. (*Comes down steps.*) I just mean, did she get home all right?

FLO. Of course she got home all right! She told me everything! (*Mrs. Potts crosses to* D. R. *lawn.*) It seems that hoodlum just abducted her! She finally had to fight him off and *walk* home. The next time you take in tramps, Helen Potts, I'll thank you to keep them on your side of the yard!

MRS. POTTS. Have you heard from Alan?

FLO. No.

MRS. POTTS. Where's the young man?

FLO. I know where he should be—in the penitentiary! And that's where he's going if he shows up around here again! (*Rosemary enters from front door.*)

ROSEMARY. (*In front doorway.*) Has anyone seen Howard?

FLO. Howard?

MRS. POTTS. (*Surprised.*) Why, no, Rosemary!

ROSEMARY. (*Nervous and uncertain—comes out on porch.*) He said he might be around this morning. (*Starts in—stops.*) Mrs. Potts, I'm . . . er . . . storing my summer clothes in the attic. . . . Could you help me a minute?

MRS. POTTS. Of course, Rosemary. (*She looks at Flo, then starts in front door.*)

ROSEMARY. (*Darting back inside front door.*) Besides, I'd like someone to talk to.

FLO. She's been running around the house all morning like a chicken with its head cut off. Something's up! (*She crosses to Millie, gives a little signal to Millie to keep quiet about Madge.*) Millie! (*She exits through front door. Now we hear the morning voices of Irma and Christine, coming by for Rosemary.*)

IRMA. (*Coming on from* L. *alley.*) Girl, I hope Rosemary is ready. I promised the principal that I'd be there early to help with registration. (*She crosses* D. *to* R. C. *lawn.*)

CHRISTINE. (*Follows Irma on from* L. *alley, stops at* L. C. *lawn.*) How do I look, Irma?

IRMA. It's a cute dress. Let me fix it in the back. (*Irma adjust the hang of the dress as Christine turns her back.*)

CHRISTINE. I think a teacher should dress up first day of school, to give the students a good first impression.

IRMA. (*Crosses to porch.*) Good morning, Millie! (*Christine follows to* U. L. *of armchair.*)

MILLIE. Hi.

IRMA. (*Opens front door.*) Is Rosemary ready?

MILLIE. Go on up if you want to. (*Irma starts in front door and is stopped by Christine saying:*)

CHRISTINE. (*To Millie.*) We missed seeing Madge on the picnic last night. (*Millie does not answer.*)

IRMA. (*Gives Christine a significant look.*) Come on, Christine. (*They go inside front door. Bomber rides on, from* L. *alley, gets off his bicycle, throws a paper on Mrs. Potts' steps, then on Flo's back porch. Then he climbs up on Mrs. Potts' porch so he can look across into Madge's room.*)

BOMBER. Hey, Madge! Wanta go dancin'? Let me be next, Madge!

MILLIE. You shut up, crazy.

BOMBER. (*Jumps down—crosses* D. C.) My brother seen 'em parked under the bridge. Alan Seymour was lookin' for 'em all over town. I knew she liked guys. (*He sees Alan approaching off beyond the Owens house, and leaves quickly out* L. *alley.*)

MILLIE. (*Not aware that Alan is approaching.*) Some day I'm really gonna kill that ornery bastard. (*Alan enters* D. R. *She turns and sees him.*) Hi, Alan! Madge got home all right. She finally had to walk all the way. (*Alan crosses* L. *to* C. *Millie rises, crosses* L. *to* D. L. *of steps.*)

ALAN. Hal drove her home. Could I see her, Millie?

MILLIE. (*Crosses* U. *to* R. C. *lawn. Calls up to Madge's window.*) Madge! Alan's here! (*Back to Alan.*) It'll probably take her a few minutes.

ALAN. Sure. (*Crosses and sits on porch corner.*)

MILLIE. (*She sits on the stump facing him.*) I . . . I always liked you, Alan. Didn't you know it?

ALAN. (*With some surprise.*) Like me?

MILLIE. (*Nods her head.*) It's awfully hard to show someone you like them, isn't it?

ALAN. (*With just a little bitterness.*) It's easy for *some* people.

MILLIE. (*Turns away.*) It makes you feel like such a sap. I don't know why.

ALAN. (*Crosses to her* R. *Rather touched.*) I . . . I'm glad you like me, Millie.

MILLIE. I don't expect you to do anything about it. I just wanted to tell you. (*Howard comes bustling on through the gate, from* R. *alley, very upset. He addresses Millie.*)

HOWARD. (*To* D. C. *lawn.*) I got to see Rosemary. Is she up in her room?

MILLIE. Hi, Howard. (*Rises, crosses* D. L. *of stump. Alan crosses* u. *by Mrs. Potts' steps.*)

HOWARD. (*Just one thing on his mind. Crosses* D.) Uh . . . I'd like to see her, please. I think she's expecting me. (*Crosses* u. *on porch to front door.*)

MILLIE. (*Crosses to* C.) You better holler at the bottom of the stairs—(*Howard is about to go in the front door, but turns back at this.*) 'cause all the others are up there, too.

HOWARD. The others?

MILLIE. Mrs. Potts and Miss Kronkite and Miss Schoenwalder.

HOWARD. Oh. I was gonna telephone her but then I thought I better come over, because you see, this is the beginning of my busy season and ——

ROSEMARY. (*Calling from inside house.*) Howard!

HOWARD. Huh?

ROSEMARY. (*Inside, to all the women.*) He's here! (*We hear a joyful babble of women's voices from inside. Howard gives one last pitiful look at Millie, then goes in front door. Millie follows him in and Alan is left alone in the yard. After a moment, Madge comes out the kitchen door.*)

MADGE. (*By bench.*) Hello, Alan. (*Her face is sad and she looks a little guilty.*)

ALAN. (*Very moved by seeing her.*) Madge!

MADGE. I . . . I'm awfully sorry.

ALAN. (*Crosses* R.) Madge, whatever happened . . . it wasn't your fault. I know what Hal's like when he's . . . But I've got Hal taken care of now! He won't be bothering you any more! (*Crosses* D. L. *to* D. L. *of stump.*)

MADGE. (*Crosses to him.*) Alan? What do you mean?

ALAN. I didn't feel like telling your mother about it yesterday, but at school I spent half of my life getting him out of jams. I knew he'd had a few tough breaks, and I tried to feel sorry for

65

him. But this is the thanks I get. There's no use pampering him any more.

MADGE. (*Concerned, but trying not to show it.*) Where is he? I mean, is he all right?

ALAN. Don't worry about Hal! He's all right. And I'll take it on myself to offer you his official good-bye!

MADGE. (*Turning quickly to him. This is a jolt to her.*) Good-b ——? Is he gone?

FLO. (*Running out kitchen door. Madge crosses to shed door.*) Madge! (*And noticing Alan for the first time. She crosses to* D. L. *of stump.*) Alan, I didn't know you were here! (*Mrs. Potts comes hurrying out of the front door excited and smiling.*)

MRS. POTTS. Flo! Flo! (*Mrs. Potts is followed closely by Irma, Christine, Rosemary and Howard. Millie comes out of the kitchen door carrying two boxes of rice. Howard and Rosemary, she on the* L., *he carrying two suitcases, cross down to porch steps and stand, she clinging to his arm. Irma crosses* D. *to* R. *of Howard as Mrs. Potts crosses* D. *to* R. *of steps and Christine crosses* D. *to* L. *of Rosemary. They are all talking happily except for Howard, who looks bewildered, and Millie, who just looks. Millie has a handful of rice which she throws on the engaged couple. She hands the two boxes to Christine who hands one to Irma. Irma pours some rice into Mrs. Potts' hands and while they continue chattering, Irma, Christine and Mrs. Potts throw handfuls of rice over Howard and Rosemary. Millie crosses* U. *to upstage kitchen post and watches from there. Rosemary wears a beautiful going-away outfit.*)

AD LIB.:

IRMA. May all your troubles be little ones!

CHRISTINE. You're getting a wonderful girl, Howard Bevans!

IRMA. Rosemary's getting a fine man!

CHRISTINE. They don't come any better than Rosemary!

MRS. POTTS. Be happy!

IRMA. May all your troubles be little ones!

MRS. POTTS. Be happy forever and ever!

IRMA. (*Crosses* D. *to top step,* D. R. *of Rosemary.*) Girl! Are you wearing something old?

ROSEMARY. An old pair of nylons but they're as good as new.

CHRISTINE. And that's a brand new outfit she's got on. Rosemary, are you wearing something blue? I don't see it!

66

ROSEMARY. (*Daringly.*) And you're not gonna! Oh, but I don't have anything to borrow!

MRS. POTTS. Here! (*Rosemary, Irma, Christine and Howard watch Mrs. Potts as she looks for something.*)

FLO. Madge, you give Rosemary something to borrow. It'll mean good luck for you. Go on, Madge! (*She takes Alan's arm and pulls him towards the steps with her.*) Rosemary, Madge has something for you to borrow!

MADGE. (*Crossing to the group by steps.*) You can borrow my handkerchief, Miss Sydney.

ROSEMARY. Thank you, Madge. (*She takes the handkerchief.*) Isn't Madge pretty, girls? (*Hal enters D. L. from Mrs. Potts' yard and, unseen by anyone, hides in the woodshed, closing the door part way. He is barefooted.*)

IRMA and CHRISTINE. Oh, yes! Yes, indeed! (*Madge turns and leaves the group, going towards Mrs. Potts' house. She sees Hal closing the door. He signals to her to be quiet, and. closes the door. Madge turns quickly to see if anyone has seen him, then sits on the stump.*)

ROSEMARY. (*During the above.*) A girl as pretty as Madge can sail through life without a care! This all happened so fast I just can't believe it! (*Alan turns from the group to join Madge. Flo then turns and crosses towards Madge. Rosemary follows Flo.*) Mrs. Owens, I left my hot-water bottle in the closet and my curlers are in the bathroom. You and the girls can have them. I stored the rest of my things in the attic. (*Looks at Howard.*) Howard and I'll come and get 'em after we settle down. Cherryvale's not so far away. We can be good friends, same as before.

FLO. I hate to bring this up now, Rosemary, but you didn't give us much notice. Don't you know anyone who I could rent the room to?

IRMA. (*Crosses to Rosemary.*) Didn't you tell her about Linda Sue Breckenridge?

ROSEMARY. Oh, yes! Linda Sue Breckenridge—she's the sewing teacher!

IRMA. And she's a darling girl!

ROSEMARY. She and Mrs. Bendix had a fight. Mrs. Bendix wanted to charge her twenty cents for her orange juice in the morning and none of us girls ever paid more'n fifteen. Did we, girls?

67

IRMA. No! I never did! Who-
ever heard of such a thing!

CHRISTINE. No! Never! I
wouldn't! I never heard of such
a thing! Twenty cents!

CHRISTINE. No! Never! I wouldn't! I never heard of such a
thing! Twenty cents!
ROSEMARY. Irma, you tell Linda Sue to get in touch with Mrs.
Owens.
FLO. Thank you, Rosemary. (*Rosemary turns and looks at How-
ard adoringly.*)
HOWARD. Rosemary, we better hurry. I still have to pick up
the license.
ROSEMARY. (*Embracing Irma and Christine who cross to her.*)
Good-bye, girls! We've had some awfully jolly times together!
(*Flo motions to Madge, telling her to get up and prepare to say
good-bye. Madge rises. Howard turns to Mrs. Potts as Rosemary
crosses to Alan and Madge. Millie crosses D. to D. R. lawn.*)
MRS. POTTS. Good-bye, Howard.
ROSEMARY. (*Pushing Madge's head down on Alan's shoulder.*)
I know you're both going to be just as happy as Howard and I
will be. (*Rosemary turns and crosses R. to Mrs. Potts. Flo speaks
quickly to Alan.*)
FLO. Alan, will you help with the bags. (*Alan hurriedly takes one
of the suitcases from Howard who is crossing to C.*)

ROSEMARY. You've been a
wonderful friend, Mrs. Potts.
MRS. POTTS. I wish you all
sorts of happiness, Rosemary.
ROSEMARY. (*Embracing her.*)
Millie, you're going to be a
famous author some day and
I'll be so proud I knew you!
MILLIE. Thanks, Miss Sydney.

HOWARD. (*To Alan.*) A
man's gotta get married sometime.
ALAN. Of course.
HOWARD. And folks'd rather
do business with a married
man.

(*No one speaks for a moment. Finally Howard turns to Rose-
mary.*)
HOWARD. All set?
ROSEMARY. And rarin' to go! (*A sudden thought.*) But where
are we goin'?
HOWARD. (*After an awkward pause.*) I got a cousin. He and

his wife run a tourist camp in the Ozarks, but I don't know whether ——

ROSEMARY. Oh, I love the Ozarks! (*She grabs Howard's arm and pulls him off alley* R. *Alan carries the suitcase off after them. Irma, Christine, Mrs. Potts and Millie follow them, all throwing rice and calling after them.*)

ALL. (*As they go off alley* R.) The Ozarks are lovely this time of year! Be happy! May all your troubles be little ones! You're getting a wonderful girl! You're getting a wonderful man!

FLO. (*Crosses to Madge.*) Madge, you've just got to talk to me! What happened last night, Madge? You haven't told me a word! (*Madge does not answer.*)

ROSEMARY. (*Off* R.) Mrs. Owens, aren't you going to say good-bye?

FLO. (*Calling.*) I will in a minute! (*Back to Madge.*) What did Alan say? Was he upset?

MADGE. I don't know, Mom.

ALAN. (*Appearing in the alley* R.) Mrs. Owens!

FLO. (*Crosses to* C. *Madge follows to her* L.) Now don't budge from this spot until I get back. I'll bring Alan right back. (*She starts off.*)

MRS. POTTS. (*Appearing in alley.*) Come on, Flo! I never thought she'd do it! (*Flo and Mrs. Potts go off alley* R.)

MADGE. (*As Hal opens the shed door, she crosses* L. *to meet him* U. L. *of stump. They crouch down. She holds his arms.*) Hal! What happened?

HAL. Baby, I'm in a bad jam! Seymour had his old man set the cops on my tail!

MADGE. Honest? How did you get away?

HAL. I had to knock one of the cops cold and swim the river!

MADGE. Oh! What can you do?

HAL. I can get out of town. There's a freight train by pretty soon. I've got to give up that job before I even get started.

MADGE. Oh, Hal. (*Offstage we hear good-byes being shouted and Howard's Chevrolet driving away. Alan and Flo enter alley* R. *Madge and Hal rise.*)

FLO. Alan! (*She crosses* D. L. *to Madge.*)

ALAN. (*Crosses* D. *to* D. C.) What are you doing here?

HAL. (*Crossing to Alan.*) You lied, kid! You told the cops I swiped your lousy car and that was a lousy lie, kid!

69

ALAN. What'd you expect me to do? You better get out of town if you know what's good for you.

HAL. I'll go when I'm ready.

ALAN. No, you won't. (*Shoving Hal.*) You're going now! (*Mrs. Potts appears in alley* R., *comes* D. *by porch. Millie comes in alley* R., *stands near kitchen door. Irma and Christine come in alley* R., *stand by gate.*)

HAL. (*Throwing Alan off to* R.) Now, look, Seymour, I don't want to fight with you. You're the only friend I ever had.

ALAN. I'm not your friend any more. You saw another pretty girl and you had to add her to your list!

HAL. That's not so! (*Madge runs to post of the porch by kitchen —Flo to her* L. *Alan springs at Hal's throat but Hal breaks the hold. Alan grabs him again but Hal swings him around and pins his arms behind him, throwing him to his knees.*)

ALAN. Let go of me! Let go of me!

HAL. (*Forces Alan to his knees.*) You've had enough, kid! (*He releases Alan, who is in tears. Alan pulls himself up and crosses to Mrs. Potts' stairs where he lies on the steps, hiding his shame.*)

FLO. (*Crossing* L. *to* D. L. *of stump.*) Alan, are you all right?

MILLIE. (*Dashing across her path—to trellis.*) Mom! Don't!

HAL. (*Goes to Madge who has come* D. *by porch.*) Gee, Baby, I guess everything's changed now.

MADGE. Where are you going?

HAL. I'll can it to Tulsa in a couple of hours. They give me a job there at the Hotel Mayo, hoppin' bells. Baby, would you come with me? Run upstairs and grab some things. (*Flo crosses* R. *to* C. *during this, slowly, fearfully.*)

FLO. (*Calls softly.*) Madge!

HAL. I know it sounds crummy, but they always let me use a little room, and we could share it. (*Madge does not answer.*) I could save my dough and maybe we could buy a little house or a farm even. Come on, Baby. (*Madge pulls her hand away from his and turns* R.) Is this as far as it goes? Is this as far as it ever goes with me? (*Now we hear a police siren off* R. *Hal runs up to corner of house,* R. *of front door, looking ff* R. *Millie runs* R. *up steps to far* R. *on porch. Flo runs to Madge. Irma and Christine exit hurriedly by* L. *alley. Hal runs down to Madge, grabs her hand and pulls her away from Flo to* C. *on the run.*) Baby, kiss me good-bye! (*Madge breaks away from him to* D. L. *of stump as Hal continues*

U. to U. C. *lawn and we hear a train whistle of an approaching freight. Hal looks off at the train and then runs* D. *to* R., *looking at Madge, whose back is turned to him. Flo runs to* D. L. *of steps.*) Baby, I gotta go! You love me, don't you?

MADGE. What good is it if I do?

HAL. (*Beseeching.*) Look, Baby, I'm a poor bastard, and I gotta claim what's mine! And you're mine, Baby! You're the only real thing I ever had—ever! Baby, kiss me good-bye! (*He crosses* D. *to* U. R. *of stump. Madge turns and throws herself into his arms and they kiss violently. The train whistle is heard loudly, very close now. Hal breaks the kiss and holding her hands, looking down into her face.*) I feel like a freak to say this, but—I love you! (*He pulls himself away, runs up to corner of kitchen porch, holding the post, glances off at the train, looks back at Madge once more.*) Good-bye! (*He turns and says this as he leaps the fence and dashes off alley* R. *Mrs. Potts exits* D. R. *as we hear police siren approach and stop off* R., *door slam. Madge crosses* D. L. *stumblingly to shed door.*)

MADGE. (*Stumbles* L. *to shed.*) Oh, Mom!

FLO. Why did this have to happen to you?

MADGE. I *do* love him! I *do!*

FLO. Madge, I hope that's not so!

MADGE. Why didn't I know it before he was gone? Why didn't someone tell me?

MILLIE. He got on the train. (*Train whistle is heard in distance.*)

MADGE. (*A cry of deep regret. Crosses* R. *to steps.*) Oh . . . now I'll never see him again.

FLO. (*Crosses to Madge's* L.) Madge, believe me, that's for the best.

MADGE. Oh, no, Mom . . . no!

FLO. (*Holds Madge.*) At least you didn't marry him.

MADGE. (*Holding Flo's hands tight around her.*) I would have . . . I would have. Oh, Mom, what can you do with the love you feel? Where is there you can take it?

FLO. (*Beaten and defeated.*) I . . . I never found out. (*Madge throws off Flo and goes into the house through front door, crying. Mrs. Potts returns* D. R., *carrying Hal's boots. She puts them on the porch by the beach chair.*)

MRS. POTTS. The police found these on the river bank. (*She sees Flo looking after Madge.*) Flo!

71

ALAN. (*Rises, comes down Mrs. Potts' stairs to bottom step.*)
Girls have always liked Hal. Months after he left the fraternity,
they still called. "Is Hal there?" "Does anyone know where Hal's
gone?" Their voices always sounded so forlorn.

FLO. (*Crosses* U. *to* C.) Alan, come and have supper tonight.
I'll make all the things you like—sweet potato pie ——

ALAN. (*Crosses* D. *and* R. *to stump.*) I'll be gone, Mrs. Owens.

FLO. Gone?

ALAN. (*Crosses* R. *to* D. L. *of steps.*) Dad's been wanting me to
take him up to Michigan on a fishing trip. I've been stalling him,
but now I ——

FLO. You'll be back before you go to school, won't you?

ALAN. I'll be back Christmas, Mrs. Owens.

FLO. Christmas! Alan, go inside and say good-bye to Madge!

ALAN. Madge is beautiful. Did I think I could spend the rest of
my life just looking at her?

FLO. Alan, see her one more time!

ALAN. (*His mind is made up.*) No! I'll be back Christmas. I'll
stop in and . . . say hello. (*He runs off* D. R.)

FLO. (*A cry of loss.—She crosses* D. *to* L. *of steps.*) Alan!

MILLIE. (*Running to* U. *of beach chair.*) Good-bye, Alan! (*She
waves.*) Good-bye, Alan! (*Mrs. Potts crosses* L. *to below stump.*)

FLO. (*In a flat voice.*) Millie, you'll be late for school.

MILLIE. Gee, I almost forgot. (*Picks up her notebook from beach
chair. Crosses to* U. *of steps.*) I'm never going to fall in love.

MRS. POTTS. Wait till you're a little older, Millie-girl, before
you say that.

MILLIE. When I get out of college I'm going to New York, and
I'll write novels that'll shock people right out of their senses. I'll
become so great and famous . . . I'll never have to fall in love.

FLO. You be just as great and famous as you want to be. Now
go on to school. (*Millie starts out* R.*—stops* R. *of steps.*)

BOY'S VOICE. (*Off* R.) Hey, Goon girl!

MILLIE. (*Looking off* R.) Poopdeck McCullough! He thinks he's
so smart.

FLO. Keep peace and let him think so.

BOY'S VOICE. (*Off* R.) Hey, Goon girl! Come kiss me! I wanna
be sick! Ha! Ha! Ha!

MILLIE. If he thinks he can get by with that, he's crazy! (*Looks
around for a weapon, runs up on lawn, finds a stick by porch,*

runs down to corner of porch, stops, looks at the stick, changes her mind, throws the stick down disdainfully and as she exits gracefully.) See you this evening. *(Millie exits* D. R.*)*

FLO. *(After a moment.)* Helen, you liked the young man, didn't you?

MRS. POTTS. With just Mama and me in the house I'd got so used to things as they were—occasionally a hairpin on the floor . . . and the smell of Mama's medicines. Then he walked through the door and clomped through the tiny rooms as if he was still outdoors. There was a man in the house, and it seemed good.

FLO. I know, but ——

MRS. POTTS. And that reminded me, I'm a woman. And that seemed good, too. *(Flo turns away abruptly. Madge enters from front door. She has changed her dress, carries a coat and a small suitcase.)*

MADGE. Mom!

FLO. *(Without turning.)* You'd better hurry, darling. You don't want to be late to work.

MADGE. Mom, please don't get mad. I'm not doing this for spite but ——

FLO. *(Turns.)* Madge!

MADGE. I'm going to Tulsa, Mom.

FLO. What?

MADGE. I know how you feel, but I don't know what else to do.

FLO. *(Crosses to steps.)* Madge—Alan's coming back at Christmas time. He's going to take you to the dance at the Country Club. He's going to forget the whole thing and ——

MADGE. I have to go, Mom.

FLO. *(Frantic.)* Madge!

MRS. POTTS. *(Restraining Flo.)* Now, Flo . . .

FLO. Now, Madge, listen to what I've got to say!

MADGE. My bus leaves in a few minutes, Mother.

FLO. Maybe you think you love him now, but in a few years you'll hate the day he set foot on our porch!

MADGE. He needs me, Mom.

FLO. He needs you because he's no good! He'll never be able to support you. And when he does have a job he'll spend all his money on drink! I know! And after a while there'll be other women!

MADGE. I guess you don't love someone because he's perfect.

73

FLO. (*Sinking down on her knees.*) Darling, even if you do love him, try to forget it! Try!

MADGE. (*Pulls away.*) It's no use, Mom. (*We hear the sound of a hot-rod off* R.)

FLO. Oh, God! Oh, God! (*The hot-rod slows down close off* R. *and we hear some boys yelling to Madge.*)

BOYS' VOICES. Hey, Madge! Hi, Beautiful! Come on, get in! Yeah, come on, Madge!

MRS. POTTS. (*Crosses* L. *and up to* U. L. *lawn.*) Who are those boys?

MADGE. Some of the gang in their hot-rods—just kids. (*She crosses quickly to* C. *and* U. *to gate. Flo runs up along porch calling her.*)

FLO. Madge! Madge! (*Madge stops, puts down bag, coat and hat, crosses to Mrs. Potts and embraces her, her eyes filling with tears.*)

MADGE. Mrs. Potts, take care of Mom for me, will you? (*She turns and looks at Flo who is weeping bitterly. She crosses to Flo who stands on the porch edge. Madge and Flo embrace.*) I'll write, Mom. Mom, don't worry. I've got some money I've been saving and there are lots of jobs in Tulsa. I can always work. (*Flo still looks bitterly unhappy. Madge puts her head against her.*) Oh, Mother! Tell Millie I never meant it all those times I said I hated her. Tell her I've always been very proud that I had such a smart sister. (*She pulls away from Flo who holds her hands until both their arms are outstretched and Madge has to pull hard to break away. Madge looks at her mother for a moment then crosses* U., *picks up her things and walks determinedly off* R. *alley. Flo runs to the gate in a frenzy.*)

FLO. Helen! Helen! could I stop her? (*Mrs. Potts grabs Flo's arm and stops her as she reaches the gate.*)

MRS. POTTS. Could anyone have stopped you, Flo?

FLO. (*Turns and looks at Mrs. Potts for a long moment.*) There are so many things I wanted to tell her!

MRS. POTTS. Let her learn them for herself, Flo.

VOICE. (*Off* L.) Helen!

MRS. POTTS. All right, Mama. (*She pats Flo encouragingly, turns and starts toward her house.*)

CURTAIN

74

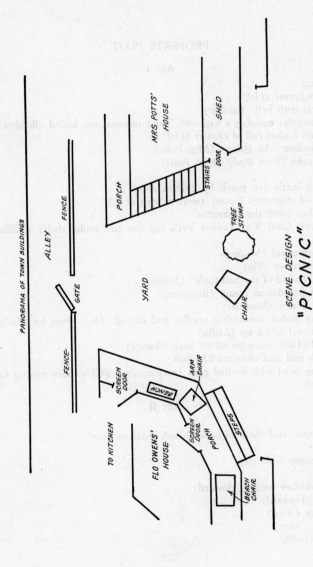

SCENE DESIGN

"PICNIC"

75

PROPERTY PLOT

Act I

Off L.:
Trash barrel (Hal)
Bicycle with bell (Bomber)
On bicycle: newsboy's bag with Tulsa newspapers, folded (Bomber)
Clothes basket full of clothes (Hal)
1 chocolate cake (prop) (Mrs. Potts)
Leaf rake (from shed) (Mrs. Potts)
On:
1 milk bottle (on porch by kitchen door)
Pack of cigarettes (open) (next to step at R.)
Matches (with the cigarettes)
Souvenir Civil War Yankee Vet's cap (on nail under shelf) (Millie)
Off R.:
Turkish towel (Madge)
Manicure set (Flo)
Book "Ballad of the Sad Cafe" (Millie)
Jar of foundation cream (Rosemary)
Hand mirror (Rosemary)
Sewing basket containing needles and thread (Flo), dress for Madge
Bath towel rolled up (Millie)
Towel (Hal) (to wipe oil off back offstage)
Sketch pad and charcoal (Millie)
Mixing bowl with deviled eggs (mayonnaise) and wooden mixing fork
(Flo)

Act II

Set:
Sketchpad and charcoal under beach chair on porch
Strike:
Newspaper from steps
Off L.:
Full whiskey bottle (Howard)
Cigar (Howard)
Ice pick (Alan)
Apron (Alan)
Cake (Millie)

Set:
Stick by porch R.
Strike:
Clothing left on
Close front door

SCENE 2

Check:
Position of stick
Set:
Open front door
Milk bottle by bench (as in Act I)
Off L.:
Bicycle with bell and newspaper bag (Bomber)
Folded newspapers (2) (Bomber)
Shopping bag (Christine)
Manila envelope (Irma)
Blanket (Hal)
Off R.:
2 boxes of rice
Looseleaf notebook (Millie)
School textbook (Millie)
2 suitcases (Howard)
1 suitcase (Madge)
Hat and coat (Madge)
Handkerchief (Madge)

NOTE: After curtain get Hal's boots and place at entrance D. R.

New TITLES

LOOK: WE'VE COME THROUGH
SEQUEL TO A VERDICT
THE SPIRAL STAIRCASE
TELEMACHUS
THAT'S WHERE THE TOWN'S GOING
THE THRACIAN HORSES
THE BACHELOR AND THE BOBBY-SOXER
CALL ME BY MY RIGHTFUL NAME
BORAK
DIANA DOES IT
DRUMS UNDER THE WINDOWS
THE 49TH COUSIN
IMPROMPTU
THREE RINGS FOR MICHELLE

● *Write for information*

DRAMATISTS PLAY SERVICE, INC.

14 East 38th Street   New York 16, N. Y.